WELCOME TRAVEL GUIDE

THE THREE CITIES

Vittoriosa, Senglea, Cospicua

The Maritime City: Vittoriosa (*Birgu*) from the air

WELCOME TRAVEL GUIDE

THE THREE CITIES

Vittoriosa, Senglea, Cospicua

John Manduca

with watercolours by
Cecily Napier

Publishers Enterprises Group (PEG) Ltd

Published by
Publishers Enterprises Group (PEG) Ltd,
P.E.G. Building
UB7, Industrial Estate,
San Gwann SGN 09, Malta

http://www.peg.com.mt
E-mail: contact@peg.com.mt

First published 2005

ISBN: 99909-0-401-4

By the same author

WELCOME GUIDE to City of Mdina and Rabat (2003)
WELCOME GUIDE to Malta & Gozo (2003)

THE BONHAM-CARTER DIARIES (2004)
WHO'S WHO (1987)
ANTIQUE MALTESE CLOCKS (Ed)
ANTIQUE FURNITURE IN MALTA (Ed)

Printed by PEG Ltd, Malta

For those who labour
to preserve
our heritage

'Walled Towns are unique inheritances from times long past and should be treasured, maintained and safeguarded from neglect, damage and destruction and passed on into perpetuity as irreplaceable Timestones of History.' *

---

* Declaration adopted at the 8th Symposium of the WALLED TOWNS FRIENDSHIP CIRCLE held in Piran, Slovenia, on 24 September, 1998, and endorsed by various European Heads of State including President Emeritus, Ugo Mifsud Bonnici, of Malta. Dr Mifsud Bonnici resides in the walled City of Cospicua

Acknowledgments

Several of my friends and colleagues helped with this WELCOME GUIDE. Among these is Lorenzo Zahra whose knowledge of and love for Vittoriosa is unsurpassed, and who was generous enough to share some of his knowledge with me. Lorenzo Zahra is one of the founder members and Secretary of the Vittoriosa Historic and Cultural Society which had done more than anyone I know to preserve the treasures and beauty of the City. Eric Parnis has also been most helpful with proof-reading, and my children and grandchildren have come to my rescue on numerous occasions. As usual, my wife has been most supportive, and the Publishers, Publishers Enterprises Group (PEG) Ltd, encouraging and helpful.

The map of Malta is by the Survey and Planning Unit of the Malta Environment and Planning Authority, while Polidano Press Ltd were responsible for the other six plans.

I am most grateful to Cecily Napier for once again producing charming watercolours, which embellish this publication - as was the case with the other WELCOME GUIDES, 'Malta & Gozo', and 'City of Mdina & Rabat'.

Various leading photographers have supplied pictures for this publication. Among these are the Dowager Marchesa Cassar De Sain, Alistair Harvey, Peter Bartolo Parnis, Fondazzjoni Patrimonju Malti, Richard Ellis Ltd and Eric Parnis, and I am indebted to them all. I am also grateful to Anthony Portelli and other officials of the Malta Tourism Authority for their assistance.

Contents

List of Illustrations

Watercolours

Photographs

Maps and Plans

A Word of Introduction

The Three Cities - Vittoriosa, Senglea and Cospicua - which lie to the southeast of Valletta, on the other side of the Grand Harbour are among the island's hidden treasures. They were devastated during the Second World War when Britain and Malta stood side by side in one of the longest sieges in history. This resulted in the loss of many treasures, but, fortunately, many remain.

They had also been in the forefront in the Great Siege of 1565, when a Turkish armada invaded the island and was defeated by the Knights of the Order of St John and by the people of the island.

From the earliest days, life in Malta was centred mainly round the shores of the Grand Harbour, so that the chequered history of Malta is the history of these ancient walled cities. Neglected for many years, the Three Cities may not yet be a major attraction to the average tourist. There are few restaurants and hotels, but this should attract the more adventurous visitor. Meanwhile, after years of indifference, the Three Cities are undergoing a renaissance, and a good start has already been made.

This is especially true of Vittoriosa, which is set to become one of the prizes sought after by the discerning visitor. The Castle of St Angelo, the Maritime Museum, the Inquisitor's Palace and the Parish Churches are all outstanding. Its waterfront and marina is impressive, and the massive fortifications which enclose the whole of 'Cottonera', (as the area is called), can hold their own anywhere in the world. They are Heritage Sites of the first order.

I have included short descriptions of the Grand

Harbour, the Fortifications, and The Great Siege of 1565, since they are all essential to a proper understanding of the Three Cities and their history.

This WELCOME GUIDE aims at making your visit both pleasant and interesting; it seeks to reduce the hassle which sometimes accompanies a visit to territory not previously explored.

The plans and maps will help, and so should the photographs and delightful watercolours.

JOHN MANDUCA

'Beaulieu'
Città Vecchia, Malta

December, 2004

Cradle of History

Napoleon got it right when he said that a country's geography makes its history. Malta is what the seas and its magnificent harbours have made her. In the Middle of the Mediterranean Sea, giving seafarers safe and deep anchorage, its strategic position also made it the object of rival ambitions, and attracted the covetous eyes of the great maritime powers. In turn, Malta has greeted the Phoenicians, the Carthaginians, the Romans, the Arabs, Normans, Spaniards, the international Order of St John, the French and for some two hundred years, the British. The islands became independent in 1964.

At the centre of events, Vittoriosa (also known as *Birgu*) was for long the only sea-faring town in the Maltese archipelago. As such, the town attracted all those who wanted control of the shipping lanes in the Middle Sea. Its early history is lost in the mist of time, but it is certain that a temple-fortress – the Castle of St Angelo – dominated the harbour from ancient times; Birgu was its suburb. Its sister towns Senglea (*L-Isla*) and Cospicua (*Bormla*), developed later, grew alongside Birgu and shared many of the triumphs and disasters of the Maritime City. The area is known as Cottonera, and its inhabitants have well-defined characteristics, and despite being ruled by many nations have detained an individuality of their own – even in their accent. The Three Cities are all walled towns.

The Phoenicians (1450-550 B.C.)

The sea-faring Phoenicians were attracted by Malta's harbours and found refuge here. They are said to have built a temple to their goddess Astarte, the 'Giver of Fertility'. The Roman, Diodorus Siculus (325-260 B.C.) recorded that 'The Phoenicians found this a place of refuge from the excellence of its harbour, and its situation in the middle of the sea.'

The Carthaginians (550-216 B.C.)
& The Romans (216 B.C. – A.D. 870)

Next came their offsprings, the Carthaginians, who used the harbour during the two Punic Wars when the great Hannibal challenged the might of the Roman Empire. The Carthaginians left behind the foundation of the Maltese language which has since absorbed many words of Roman origin, mainly Italian which was an official language here until 1934. Malta is now a bi-lingual country with Maltese and English being official languages.

When Carthage was destroyed, the Romans took over and the goddess Astarte became the goddess Juno. The historian Quininium wrote: 'I believe the temple of Juno could be counted not only among the great but also among the magnificent temples of this divinity.' The Mediterranean became a Roman Lake.

It was during this period that Paul of Tarsus (St Paul) on his way to face trial in Rome was shipwrecked here in A.D. 60. The Acts of the Apostles record that the Maltese showed him, 'no small kindness; for kindling a fire they refreshed us all.' Paul stayed in Malta for three months and converted the islanders to Christianity.

The Arabs (A.D. 870-1090)

In the year 870, the Arabs destroyed the temple and built a Castle in its stead. Muslim ships with their green banner used Malta as a base for attacks on Italian cities in the south of the peninsula. The Arabs introduced a number of new crops including cotton, and are said to have brought with them, the orange, the lemon and the pomegranate. They also left a fusion of a kindred idiom into the Punic language of the Maltese.

The Normans (A.D. 1090-1194)

The Normans, under Count Roger, a kinsman of William and the Conqueror, and a member of the Hauteville family, ousted the Arabs. They took over the Castle, made it stronger and built a Christian chapel dedicated to the Virgin Mary. The Castle became the seat of the de Nava family during the so-called 'Spanish Period', and St Angelo became known as the *Castello a Mare* to the Aragonese and to the Castilians who followed.

The Spaniards (A.D. 1282-1530)

The Normans were succeeded by the German Emperors of the Swabian House of Hohenstaufen and by the Angevins (1266-82). In their turn the French were ousted by Peter of Aragon and Malta became the property of the Spanish Kings, held first by the Aragonese (1282-1479) and next by the Castilians (1479-1530).

Several of the great monastic Orders settled in Malta during this period – the Franciscans arriving first in 1370.

Despite protests, King Alphonse V, mortgaged the islands for 30,000 gold florins to Sicilian Viceroy, Don Antonio Cardona in 1420. When Cardona was succeeded by Don Gonslavo Monroy the Maltese had had enough. They threw Monroy out and imprisoned his wife, Donna Costanza, in the Castle of St Angelo. The King threatened to starve the Islanders but after some bargaining, peace was restored and the King was placated when the Maltese raised 30,000 florins and redeemed their island. The King visited Malta in 1430 and promised that Malta would 'be reunited in perpetuity to the Spanish Crown.'

During the early fifteen-century the Maltese islands were repeatedly attacked by Barbery pirates – 'sea wolves of the Mediterranean.' Malta's harbour became a nest for Christian corsairs, plundering no less than the Muslins. Birgu provided the arsenals and the provisions for these excursions. It remained at the centre of the events and became cosmopolitan with Venetian, Genovese, and Sicilian sailors and merchants rubbing shoulder with the Maltese inhabitants. Over the years Birgu, with its rich history, accumulated a precious and abundant artistic and cultural heritage, some of which can be enjoyed today.

The Order of St John (A.D. 1530-1798)

The promise made by the King in 1430 was broken in 1530 when the Emperor Charles V gave the Islands to the international Order of St John of Jerusalem. In return, the Emperor accepted a yearly gift of a falcon presented to his Viceroy in Sicily.

The Knights were not immediately welcomed by the Maltese nobility who were denied entry into the Order of Chivalry despite an undertaking given by the first Grand Master, Fra Philippe Villiers de L'Isle Adam.

But economically, Birgu prospered with the arrival of the Order whose members were described as 'the most remarkable body of religious warriors that the world has ever seen.' Birgu became a Citadel of the Knights, and their 'capital' city although officially the capital was Notabile (Mdina) where most of the Maltese nobility lived.

The Order relied on its naval prowess for its survival, and chose Birgu as its headquarters, because of its strategic position by the sea. They quickly fortified it, built *Auberges* and hospitals, and redeveloped it to accommodate their galley squadron. At Rhodes the knights had lived in isolation in a *Collachio* (convent) but neither Birgu (nor Valletta) had an area inhabited only by knights. All the Auberges expect that of Italy were situated in the area known as the *Collachio*.

The Three Cities achieved fame during the Great Siege of 1565 when a massive Turkish armada attacked the island for four months in a vain effort to rid themselves of a formidable enemy who had provoked 'Soleyman the Magnificence', Sultan of Turkey. Soleyman had been advised that 'until you have smoked out this nest of vipers you can do no good anywhere'. *Birgu, Senglea* and *Cospicua* bore the brunt of the siege, with men, women and children all playing their part, often acting heroically. Massive fortifications were built later making Cottonera impregnable. These massive fortifications were acclaimed all over Europe as 'a masterpiece of military architecture'.

Following the siege, the Order decided to build a new and stronger City – Valletta – and Cottonera lost some of its importance. But since the Order of St John – fearing another invasion – failed to complete Valletta as planned to include a shipyard, the galley squadron remained in Galley Creek, between Vittoriosa and Senglea. The population grew rapidly. In Birgu stood buildings devoted to the construction and repair of the Order's famous navy, and these activities ensued prosperity for The Three Cities. In 1634, the Order laid down that no more houses be built in either Vittoriosa or Senglea, and in 1666 people from the countryside were prohibited from moving to the cities, which were already overcrowded. In 1676 the dreaded plague appeared and the population of Vittoriosa was reduced by one thousand souls.

The defeat of the Turks ensured the safety of Europe, but it deprived the Order of its *raison d'etre* and many of the knights became tyrannical and dissolute.

The French (1789-1800)

In 1797 Napoleon Bonaparte wrote to his shrewd Minister Talleyrand: 'Why do we not take possession of Malta.... four hundred knights and five hundred soldiers are all that form the garrison of Valletta. The inhabitants who number one hundred thousand are friendly to us, and greatly disgusted with the knights... with the islands of Sardinia, Malta and Corfu we should be masters of the whole Mediterranean.'

Talleyrand replied: 'The Directory approves of your intentions respecting Malta.'

Napoleon informed the British Ambassador in Paris that 'Peace or War depends upon Malta.'

When Napoleon's forces arrived off the island in June 1798, Malta and Gozo were taken after little more than token resistance. The last Grand Master, Ferdinand Hompesch, a German, left the island with his immediate entourage. The mighty forts and the massive bastion fell to the French.

Initially welcomed by those who looked on the French as 'liberators', disillusion soon followed, and the Maltese rose in revolt when attempts were made to sell church property. The insurgents managed to isolate the French in Valletta, and in Cottonera. But the massive fortifications now worked against them and the Maltese could make little headway on their own. They appealed to Britain for help and though at first Nelson was reluctant to become involved, claiming that 'Sardinia was worth fifty Maltas as a Mediterranean base and hospital centre', he soon came round to the view that Malta could not remain in French hands. Nelson's ships blockaded the island and prevented food and ammunition reaching the French. British troops arrived and General Vaubois, the Commander-in-Chief surrendered and left after having occupied the island for as little over a year.

The three walled towns came to be known as *The Three*

Cities having been referred to by that name by the French in 1798, in an attempt it is said, to win the inhabitants over in those turbulent times. The stratagem failed.

The British (1800-1964)

After a great deal of manoeuvring and intrigue the Treaty of Paris was signed in 1814 placing the Maltese islands under the protection of Great Britain.

Britain had established itself as the predominant naval power and Malta increased in importance following the opening of the Suez Canal in 1869.

Malta played its part in the war of the Crimea when it became known as the 'Nurse of the Mediterranean'. Its hospitals were expanded to accommodate 20,000 patients; in fact some 80,000 servicemen passed through Malta during the war (1854-56) with Britain and France on one side and Russia on the other.

(Florence Nightingale's nursing exploits at Scutari became famous[1] and so did the Charge of the Light Brigade at Balaclava in 1854.)

During the Great War, the island's extensive naval facilities were made available to the French Fleet, which was invited by Winston Churchill, then First Lord of the Admiralty, 'to use Malta as if it were Toulon'.

Many of those living in The Three Cities found work with the Royal Navy and the Merchant navy. British warships sailed in and out of Grand Harbour and St Angelo

---

[1] Florence Nightingale arrived in Grand Harbour on the 30th October, 1854, on board the steamer *Vectis* on her way to take up her duties. Her party, nuns and nursing sisters, visited several places of interest including St John's cathedral in Valletta, before continuing their voyage to the East. At Scutari Hospital, she came across a number of Maltese physicians who had offered their services, and Florence Nightingale wrote a personal letter of thanks to a Dr Salvatore Luigi Pisani.

was the headquarters of the mighty fleet. Churchill portrays the fleet sailing to the war stations as: 'gigantic castles of steel winding their way across the misty, shining seas, like giants bowed in anxious thought.'

When war broke out in 1939, the Castle of St Angelo became H.M.S. St Angelo, and there were some 12,000 men working in the Dockyard. Malta stood in the front line and some 30,000 houses were destroyed or damaged during 3000 air raids in an area no larger than the Isle of Wight. Some 14,000 tons of bombs fell on the Island and the second great siege lasted for over two years. Food and ammunition were in short supply and the island was saved from starvation and possible surrender by ships of the Royal Navy, and by the gallant seamen manning the 'Santa Maria' convoy which reached Malta just in time with supplies. The brunt of the attacks fell on the harbour area with The Three Cities suffering horrendous damage. In April 1942, King George VI awarded Malta the George Cross 'to bear witness to a heroism and devotion to duty that will long be famous in history'. President Roosevelt sent a scroll 'to the island of Malta...alone and unafraid, one tiny flame in the darkness'.

In September 1964 the Maltese islands became independent within the Commonwealth.[2] British armed forces left the islands in 1979, and the monument outside St Lawrence Church in Vittoriosa records this event. Malta joined the European Union as a full member in 2004.

Malta now relies on light industry, its Freeport, and tourism for its livelihood. Vittoriosa and its neighbours are being 're-discovered' and coming back into the limelight.

---

[2] A meeting of the Commonwealth Heads of Government takes place in Malta in 2005, and Malta will welcome the Queen as Head of Commonwealth. As Princess Elisabeth, the Queen spent a happy time in Malta when Prince Philip was a naval officer serving with the Mediterranean Fleet.

The Grand Harbour

Malta is what the sea and her harbours have made her. The truly magnificent Grand Harbour is surrounded by the bastions of Fort St Elmo, Fort Ricasoli, and the Castle of St Angelo. There are four inner creeks – Rinella, Kalkara, Dockyard and French Creeks. All of these afford safe anchorage. The shoreline of Grand Harbour is some 16 kilometres long and it encloses 540 acres of water. Looking across the Harbour from the Upper Barracca in Valletta is a stunning sight. In the background are the 'Three Cities' of Vittoriosa ('Birgu'), Senglea ('L'Isla') and Cospicua ('Bormla'). It was this great harbour which made the island the object of fierce rivalry throughout the ages.

Elizabeth Schermerhorn writing in 1929 said:

> *'The life and colour of the Grand Harbour viewed from the lofty arcades of the Upper Barracca, make a vivid appeal to the eye and the imagination... The great port, whose mouth is hardly a quarter of a mile wide, and which runs two miles into the heart of the island is so deep that the largest ship can ride there in stormy weather without cable. The harbour waited many centuries for the Knights Hospitallers to discover its inestimable advantages as a harbour and to fortify it with batteries that could tear the strongest ship to pieces before they could enter. But they came at last, and made it so perfect that all the great powers of Europe coveted it."*

Many others have sung its praises. Samuel Taylor Coleridge, the English poet who served for some time in Malta as Private Secretary to the Civil Commissioner, Sir

Alexander Ball (1804-1805), described the *Porto Grande* as 'one of the finest in the world'. On his part, Hans Christian Andersen, Denmark's national poet, wrote in his travelogue: *A Visit to Germany, Italy and Malta (1840-41):*

> *'I heard the anchor fall and knew that we were in the harbour of Malta. I have never before seen such brilliance, either under the clear skies of Italy or in our northern winter nights. Valletta and all those proud ships here under the world's strongest fortress were only the frame for it. The setting was beautiful, one of the most beautiful I have ever seen....ships came and went, canons saluted the fortress and were in turn greeted.'*

E-Boat Attack

The Italian E-Boat and torpedo attack on Grand Harbour on the night of July 25th, 1941 was a brave exploit. The damage caused to the viaduct of the breakwater as a result is still evident as you enter Grand Harbour.

The supply position in Malta in 1941 was desperate, and it was decided to send a convoy to relieve the garrison and people. The Royal Navy lost one destroyer and one cruiser in the attempt, but six merchantmen with much

> Malta's stand during World War II reminds one of Seneca's finest play. Medea is at bay, and her old nurse, is trying to persuade her to give in. 'What's the good of going on?' she says. 'Your friends have deserted you, your own countrymen are far away, your resources are spent. *Quid jam superset?* What remains?'. *'Medea superset'* is the great answer. 'Medea Remains'. The same question was put to Malta in 1942. She gave the same answer: *'Melita superset'*
> *(The Siege Within the Walls,' Malta 1940-43* by Stewart Perowne)

needed food and stores entered Grand Harbour on the 24th July. The Italians were determined to destroy these vessels and their escorting warships by forcing their way through protective nets of Grand Harbour by means of fast motor torpedo boats and one man submarines, in reality human torpedoes.

Immediately, radar showed the approach of Italian units, the searchlights of Fort St Elmo, Tigne and Ricasoli were switched on and the shore batteries, mostly Maltese manned, opened fire. Everyone of the eighteen enemy vessels were destroyed and those trying to turn back were finished off by Hurricanes of the Royal Air Force. Not one of the ships in harbour suffered damaged.

Santa Maria Convoy

The Santa Maria Convoy which helped to save Malta and its beleaguered garrison from starvation has become part of Malta's and of naval history. On the 9th March 1942, Admiral Syfret in the "Nelson", with the "Rodney", three aircraft-carriers and thirty-two destroyers entered the Mediterranean. "Operation Pedestal" had begun.

Its object was to escort fourteen merchantmen, one of which was the tanker "Ohio", loaded with 11,000 tons of kerosene and fuel oil. The other ships in the convoy carried 85,000 tons of cargo: flour, petrol, aviation spirit, and explosives.

Some 321 kilometres from Malta, Admiral Burroughs took over and was met by a mounting crescendo of U-Boat and E-Boat attacks and wave after wave of enemy aircraft. The cruisers "Manchester" and "Cairo" were lost and so were seven merchantmen.

The "Ohio" was hit and hit again and was taken in tow by the destroyer "Penn". Twice the "Ohio" was abandoned and twice she was boarded again and taken in tow. Finally two destroyers literally held her up, on one on either side, and on Sunday 16th August[3] to the cheers of the people who lined the bastions, gallant "Ohio" entered Grand Harbour with her precious cargo.

[3] August 15th is the Feast of Santa Maria – hence the name by which the convoy came to be known.

The Order of St John

The Order of St John was founded during the time of the First Crusade to help pilgrims visiting the Holy Land. Its Constitution was sanctioned by Pope Pascal II in 1113, and the first Knight to assume the title of 'Master' – later Grand Master – was Raymond Du Puy (1125-1158). The Knights established many hospitals and because of repeated Saracen attacks developed rapidly into warrior monks "long renowned as Champions of the Cross."

Forced out of the Holy Land, Cyprus and Rhodes, the Order was befriended by the Emperor Charles V who gave them Malta and its sister island Gozo in 1530 "in order that they perform the duties of their Religion and employ their forces and arms against the perfidious enemies of Holy Faith."

The first of the twenty-eight Grand Masters who ruled in Malta was Philippe Villiers de L'Isle Adam, a Frenchman, and the last was Ferdinand von Hompesch, a German who surrendered to Napoleon in 1798.

This aristocratic Order of Chivalry, the oldest in Christendom, was divided into the following classes: Knights of Justice or Military Knights; Knights of Honour and Devotion; Knights of Magisterial Grace; Chaplains and Servants-at-Arms or Donats. Before admission into the Order, the Knights of Malta were required to produce proofs of nobility on both the father's and the mother's side of eight quarterings.

A remarkable body of religious warriors who as Gibbons remarked may have "neglected to live" but who were certainly "prepared to die in the service of the Cross."

The Order was also divided into eight Langues or

Protocol assumed great importance when the Order of St John reigned in Malta. Rules provided for every contingency. For example, if the Grand Master and the Inquisitor are both in their coaches when they meet, the Inquisitor is supposed to stop to allow the Grand Master to pass; if he is in his coach and the Grand Master is on foot, the inquisitor should make him a profound salute and continues on his way. A quarrel between the two sides occurred in the reign of Grand Master Perellos (a Spaniard, 1697-1720) when the Inquisitor's coach blocked one of the narrow street in Valletta forcing the Grand Master's coach to come to a halt. Fortunately for the Grand Master the Inquisitor's relations with the Bishop were also not happy, so that the Grand Master could and often did play one against the other.

Divisions in accordance with their nationality and each Langue had its own Auberge or Inn. The Langues were those of Provence, Auvergne, France, Italy, Aragon, England and Germany. Aragon was later divided making an eight Langue of Castile and Leon.

The Order's Head was the Grand Master who presided over the Supreme Council. This consisted of the Bishop of the Order, the Heads of each Langue, the Priors, the Conventual's Bailiffs and the Knight Grand Cross – the senior Knights of the various nationalities.

The Badge chosen by the Order around 1259 was the eight-pointed cross, commonly known as the Maltese Cross.

The Grand Masters ranked as Ruling Princes in Europe and most, if not all, of the forts, castles, churches and other landmarks you will see were built during the two hundred and sixty eight year that the "Sovereign Military Hospitaller Order of St John of Jerusalem, of Rhodes and of Malta" – to give it its full title – reigned in Malta.

On arrival in the Maltese islands, after their expulsion from Rhodes which they called the 'island of roses', the Knights were not immediately enamoured with what they saw though some of their misgivings disappeared when they settled in the *Borgo di Castello* (now Vittoriosa), lapped by the waters of the splendid harbour. For their part the Maltese, including the inhabitants of Birgu, were no better pleased with the new arrangement made without consultation by the Emperor Charles V, the most powerful monarch in the West.

Elizabeth Schermerhorn summed up the feeling of many Maltese when she wrote in 1929:

> *'To the educated and aristocratic Maltese, well-informed on local history, the memory of the imperious Order that took away parliament and free institutions, interfered with the sacred privileges of the bishopric, snobbishly refused membership to the sons of families whose titles of nobility antedated the occupation of Rhodes, and after boasting that its standard had never been lowered to any foe, surrendered the island to the French warships without a struggle, is simply not to be discussed or defended in any well-bred circles.'*

It took time for the two sides to get closer. The fact that the Knights and the Maltase had fought, valiantly, alongside each other against a common enemy helped to improve relations, which became warmer as the years went up. But they deteriorated once again when in 1798 Napoleon invaded Malta and confusion reigned; many Maltese felt betrayed.

Though there was little, if any, political liberty, the Knights brought increasing commerce to The Three Cities and to the Harbour. Fortifications, docks, warehouses, magazines, Churches and mills began to spring up as never before. There was about enough for most Maltese and for the camp followers who gathered around the Cross of St John. This increased activity, and therefore a higher standard of living followed as it did on the arrival of the British in 1800.

Of the twenty-eight Grand Masters who ruled in Malta from 1530 to 1798, twelve were French; eight Spanish; four Italian, three came from Portugal and one, Ferdinand von Hompesch, was German.

The Knights of Malta dined off silver plates and they ate well. In the seventeenth century a Frenchman gave a vivid account of their style of living. He wrote:

'I never failed to admire the quantity of the viands that were served and to wonder how so dry and barren a rock can produce such refreshments and so much game. Every day the market is full of vegetables and of almost every kind of fruit; the bread is excellent; beef and mutton of a marvellous taste. Veal and poultry are eaten at all seasons.... there is no lack of iced dishes and of snow, thanks to the efforts of the contractor who charges two sols six deniers a pound on the understanding that he supplies it all the year round. He brings it from the mountains of Sicily....'

The Head of each Langue was known as the Pillar and each had special duties assigned to the post, the French Pillar was the Grand Hospitaller. The Pillar of Provence was the Grand Commander in charge of the Treasury. The Pillar of Italy was the Grand Admiral while the Pillar of Castile was known as the Grand Chancellor. The Pillar of England bore the title of Turcopiler and was in charge of the cavalry and the military. They all settled in Vittoriosa.

The Fortifications

The Knights did not want a repetition of what had happened in Rhodes and were determined to make Malta impregnable. From 1530 up to 1798, they undertook long lines of defence and an infinite system of fortifications. Malta became and remains a treasure trove of military architecture.

Alison Hoppen, the historian wrote : *'For the student of European military history the Maltese fortifications, because of their concentration is so small an area, because of their compactness, because of the extensive survival of records connected with their construction, represent a unique opportunity for examining in detail the planning and building of large-scale defensive works.'*

In 1834, Samuel Taylor Coleridge, was impressed and said: *'the fortifications are endless. When I first walked about them, I was struck all of a heap of their strangeness, and when I began to understand a little of their purpose, I was overwhelmed with wonder.'*

In an island nineteen miles by nine, there are no less than 20 miles of fortifications.

Among the most impressive of these fortifications are the Cottonera Lines (named after the Grand Master Nicolas Cotoner, a Spaniard (1663-1680) who spent enormous sum of money to have them built.) The project received much criticism being considered too expensive, but Cotoner was undismayed and resolved to carry on with his ambitious scheme. The work continued for over ten years, and though some amendment had to be made due to shortage of funds, the works were completed in a modified but still impressive form. *(See Plan on page 38)*

Cottonera & Margherita Lines

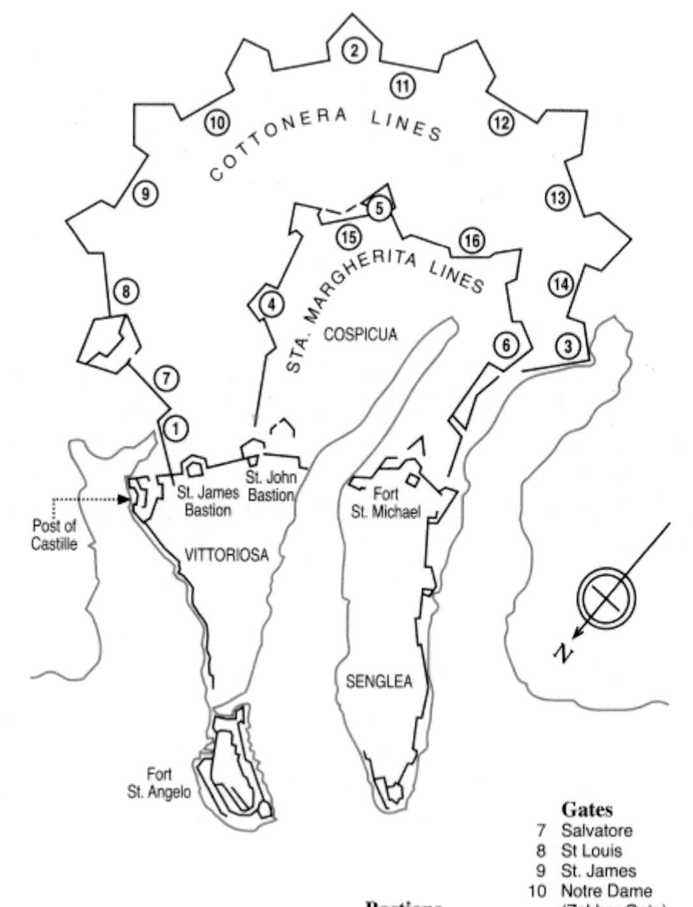

Bastions

1 St. Lawrence
2 St. Clement
3 Valperga
4 Firenzuola
5 St. Helen
6 St. Francis

Gates

7 Salvatore
8 St Louis
9 St. James
10 Notre Dame (Zabbar Gate)
11 St. Clement
12 Polverista
13 St. John
14 St. Paul
15 Verdala
16 St. Helen

Around 1630-40 a scheme was put in hand to improve the defences of Vittoriosa and of Senglea with defensive works known as the Sta Margherita Lines. Enclosed within these lines was Fort St Angelo together with Vittoriosa and Senglea. The Cottonera Lines strengthened these defences enormously and also enclosed Cospicua. The fortification may well have deterred an enemy from attempting an attack. In the centre of each curtain stands a stately gateway considered among the masterpieces of Baroque architecture. The most splendid is probably the Zabbar Gate (also known as Notre Dame Gate) with an inscription recording the gift of the works by Grand Master Cotoner surmounted by a bronze bust of the donor and surrounded by the rich carving of angels.

This was the Grand Master's most ambitious project designed to protect The Three Cities. Nicolo' Cotoner requested the skilled services of the renowned Papal Military Engineer Count Valperga, and to subsidise his huge project Cotoner levied a tax on immovable property.

The vast and magnificent Cottonera Lines extend for several miles round the three cities of Vittoriosa, Cospicua and Senglea, in a semi-circular shape. The foundation stone was laid with great solemnity on August 28th 1670 by the Grand Master. The fortifications are called after him, and consist of a fortified city with eight bastions and two demi-bastions (one of the latter is called Valperga Demi-Bastion after the name of the engineer). The Lines are 4,600 metres in length and the new fortress was considered capable of giving asylum, in case of invasion, to 40,000 people, together with their belongings and a good number of cattle.

It was during his rule and that of Gregorio Caraffa (1680-90) that the fleet of the Order and privateering came to a climax. From 1660 to 1680, ninety-eight licences were granted for corsairs sailing under the flag of the Order of St John. The wars of Candia (1645-69) and the Morea (1684-99) in which ships of the Order took part provided an ideal training ground for European naval officers, and from a practical point of view preying on Muslim trade was essential for the Orders finances' and for the Island's economy.

The Three Cities, with first-rate naval docks and facilities played a pivotal part in all this activity.

The Great Siege

Malta of Gold, Malta of Silver
Malta of Precious Metal
We shall never take you!
I am she who has decimated the galleys of the Turk –
And all the warriors of Constantinople and the Galata![4]

The Turkish attack on Malta in 1565, in what has became known as the Great Siege, was one of the most celebrated and decisive battles in the history of the western world. The outcome was of universal concern, for the future of the Christian Europe was in the balance. *'If the Turks should prevail'* remarked the Protestant Queen of England, Elisabeth I, '*it is uncertain what further peril might follow to the rest of Christendom.*'

Soleyman the Magnificent, Sultan of Turkey, who had defeated the Order of St John in Rhodes determined to take 'this cursed rock' and sent an armada of 181 galleys and 40,000 men under the command of Mustapha Pasha, Admiral Piali and the corsair Dragut. The Turkish forces included 6,000 elite Janissaries who formed the spearhead of the fighting troops, 9,000 Spahis; 4,000 Iayalars, a special cops composed of religious fanatics; Algerians and a large number of renegade Greeks and Levantines.

Opposing them, under Grand Master Jean Parisot de la Valette, 'towering up above all the others with his superb

---

[4] From a 16th Century Cypriot ballad.

The four arms of the eight-pointed Maltese Cross represent the Christian virtues: Prudence, Justice, Temperance and Fortitude, and the points the eight Beatitudes given by Christ in the Sermon of the Mount: (i) Blessed are the poor in spirit, for theirs is the Kingdom of Heaven; (ii) Blessed are the poor, for they shall possess the land; (iii) Blessed are they that mourn, for they shall be comforted; (iv) Blessed are they that hunger and thirst after justice, for they shall have their fill; (v) Blessed are the merciful for they shall obtain mercy; (vi) Blessed are the clean of heart, for they shall see God; (vii) Blessed are the peacemakers, for they shall be called the children of God; and (viii) Blessed are they that suffer persecution for justice's sake, for theirs is the Kingdom of Heaven.

majesty and bearing', were 600 Knights[5] (later increased to some 700); a garrison of 9,000, most of them Maltese, some Spanish soldiers, and Maltese civilians including women and children who tended the wounded and ensured supplies.

The Turks landed unopposed at Marsaxlokk and operations began against Fort St Elmo which was besieged for thirty-four days. Cut off from all outside help, St Elmo fell on the 23rd June when no defender remained alive. On the same day a shot fired from Fort St Angelo killed Dragut.

Repeated attacks were next launched against Fort St Michael, Fort St Angelo, Senglea and Birgu (Vittoriosa). It is estimated that over 70,000 cannon shots were fired during the siege, and under the scorching sun the shores of Grand Harbour were piled high with corpses. The hand-to-hand fighting on land and in the sea was fierce and bloody and the defence of the Knights and the Maltese

---

[5] Including one Englishman, Sir Oliver Starkey, La Vallette's trusted Latin Secretary. Two English volunteers, John Smith and Edward Stanley are said to have formed part of the relief force.

heroic: 'no war is more cruel and bloody than siege warfare.'

On the 7th September, a relief force of between 8,000 and 12,000 men reached Malta from Sicily and the Turkish forces, some 10,000 of the original armada, withdrew and returned to Constantinople. The price was high. Malta and The Three Cities were in ruins. When the relief force looked around them 'their hearts were filled with unspeakable anguish'. 250 Knights lost their lives as well as 7,000 soldiers and Maltese civilians who fought alongside the men-at-arms. And out of the original garrison of 9,000 only 600 were left capable of bearing arms.

But Malta and the rest Europe were saved.

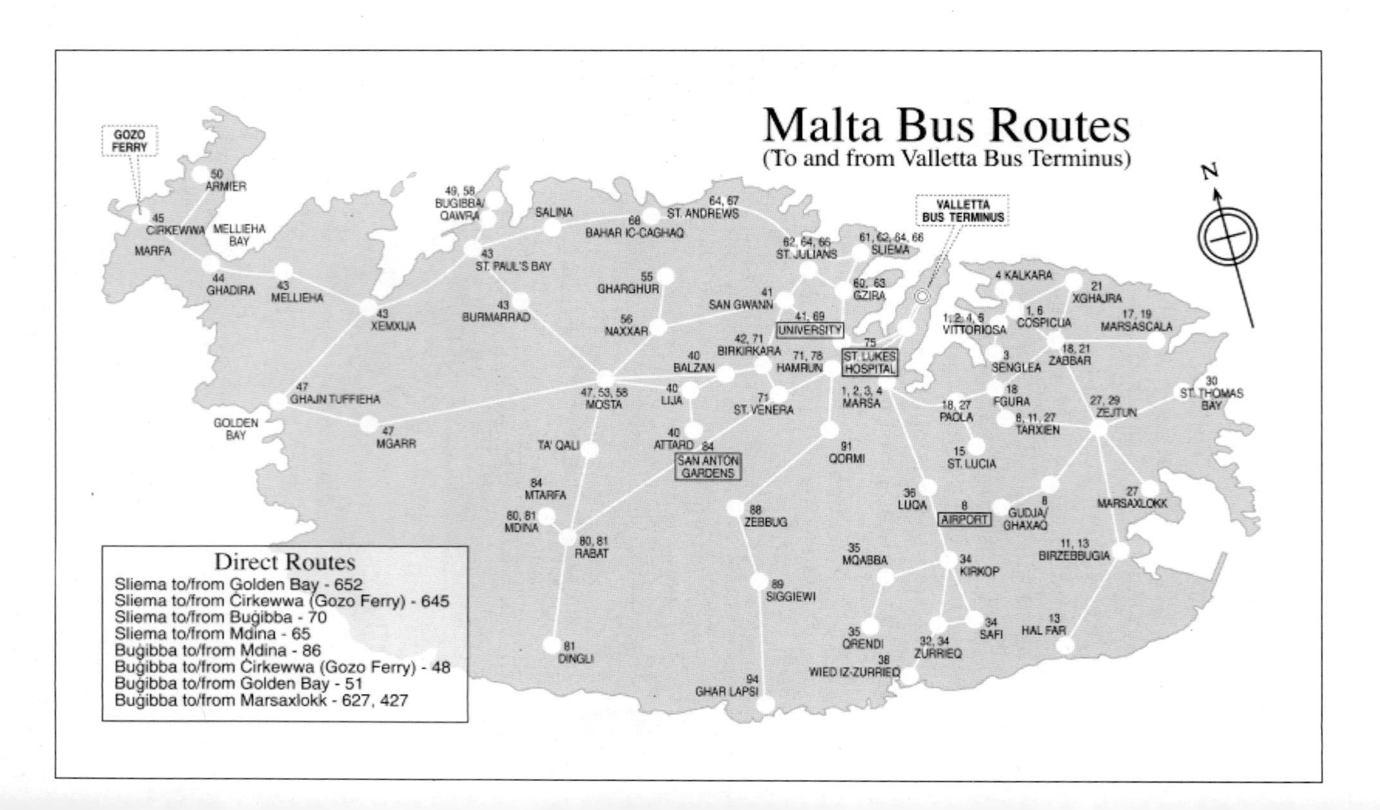
Malta Bus Routes
(To and from Valletta Bus Terminus)
N
GOZO FERRY
50 ARMIER
45 CIRKEWWA
MELLIEHA BAY
MARFA
44 GHADIRA
43 MELLIEHA
43 XEMXIJA
47 GHAJN TUFFIEHA
GOLDEN BAY
47 MGARR
49, 58 BUGIBBA/ QAWRA
43 ST. PAUL'S BAY
43 BURMARRAD
SALINA
68 BAHAR IC-CAGHAQ
64, 67 ST. ANDREWS
55 GHARGHUR
56 NAXXAR
47, 53, 58 MOSTA
TA' QALI
84 MTARFA
80, 81 MDINA
80, 81 RABAT
81 DINGLI
40 BALZAN
40 LIJA
40 ATTARD
84 SAN ANTON GARDENS
42, 71 BIRKIRKARA
41 SAN GWANN
41, 69 UNIVERSITY
62, 64, 66 ST. JULIANS
61, 62, 64, 66 SLIEMA
60, 63 GZIRA
71 ST. VENERA
71, 78 HAMRUN
75 ST. LUKES HOSPITAL
1, 2, 3, 4 MARSA
91 QORMI
88 ZEBBUG
89 SIGGIEWI
94 GHAR LAPSI
VALLETTA BUS TERMINUS
4 KALKARA
1, 2, 4, 6 VITTORIOSA
1, 6 COSPICUA
3 SENGLEA
21 XGHAJRA
17, 19 MARSASCALA
18, 21 ZABBAR
18 FGURA
18, 27 PAOLA
8, 11, 27 TARXIEN
27, 29 ZEJTUN
30 ST. THOMAS BAY
15 ST. LUCIA
36 LUQA
8 AIRPORT
8 GUDJA/ GHAXAQ
27 MARSAXLOKK
11, 13 BIRZEBBUGIA
13 HAL FAR
34 KIRKOP
34 SAFI
32, 34 ZURRIEQ
35 MQABBA
35 QRENDI
38 WIED IZ-ZURRIEQ
Direct Routes
Sliema to/from Golden Bay - 652
Sliema to/from Ċirkewwa (Gozo Ferry) - 645
Sliema to/from Buġibba - 70
Sliema to/from Mdina - 65
Buġibba to/from Mdina - 86
Buġibba to/from Ċirkewwa (Gozo Ferry) - 48
Buġibba to/from Golden Bay - 51
Buġibba to/from Marsaxlokk - 627, 427

1. One of the narrow, winding streets of Birgu, home of the original Auberge d'Angleterre

2. Entrance to the Auberge de France, scheduled to become a Museum of the Maltese language

3. The arms of England over a gateway, built in 1892, leading to the Marina in Birgu, and (*below*) a 17th century artist's impression of Valletta, Vittoriosa, Senglea and Cospicua

4. The back of the Monastery of Santa Scolastica, formerly the Hospital of the Knights, facing Salvatore Hill

5. An 18th century engraving of Grand Harbour showing Kalkara and The Three Cities.

6. A striking aerial view of the Birgu Waterfront and of The Three Cities

7. The Marina and the Parish Church of St Lawrence, on the Feast Day of the Saint

8. On guard: the Castle of St Angelo at night

9. Scamp's Palace, now the *Casino di Venezia*

10. Formerly the British Naval Bakery, and before that the Arsenal of the Galleys of the Order, this building is now the Maritime Museum

11. The Figurehead from HMS Hibernia, flagship of the British Naval Station for over fifty years, on display in the Maritime Museum

12. The Royal Navy, which used the Grand Harbour for well over two hundred years, is well represented at the Maritime Museum

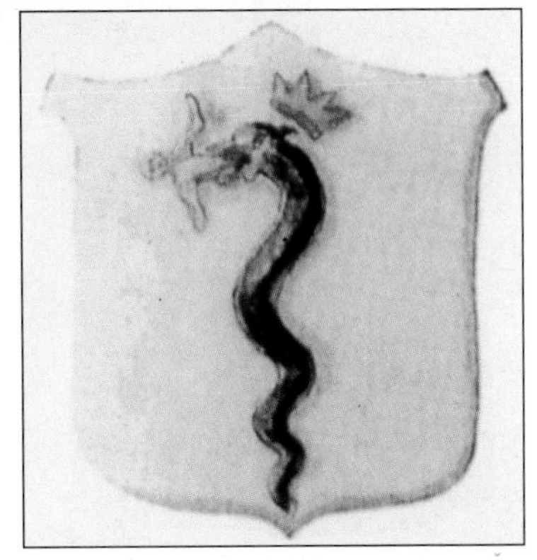

13. Coats of Arms of the Roman Inquisition and of Inquisitors who served in Malta, including Fabio Chigi (1634) who became Pope Alexander VII

14. The beautiful courtyard of the Inquisitor's Palace

15. Soleyman the Magnificent, Sultan of Turkey (1494-1566) who ordered the invasion of Malta; and (right) Jean Parisot de la Valette (1557-1567) the Grandmaster who with his Knights and the people of Malta, defended the island in a siege lasting four months

Vittoriosa (*Birgu*)

The Waterfront and Vittoriosa Marina

The Vittoriosa Waterfront, previously known as the *Marina Grande* is something special – uniquely lined as it is with imposing 16th and 17th century palaces. Recent reconstruction and repair are ensuring a renaissance for this part of the ancient city.

Vittoriosa is in the process of being 'rehabilitated' and a good start has been made with the development of the Grand Harbour Marina carried out in association with

The Birgu Waterfront

Camper & Nicholsons Marinas who have already attracted yachts from clients internationally. So far, the Marina has 214 berths for yachts between 15 and 55 metres long, and another 33 berths for larger yachts, between 30 and 100 metres long.

The waterfront stretches along the Grand Harbour between the Parish Church of St Lawrence and Fort St Angelo at the tip of the peninsula. It is especially impressive, and indeed beautiful, at night.

Having disembarked at the Bus terminus or driven by car towards or through the Gate built by the British in 1819 (observe the Royal Arms on the top) the first building of note is the Maritime Museum (formerly a British Naval Bakery which replaced the Arsenal of the Order of St John). This is well worth a visit (see page 66)

Next, you come across the Treasury building. Now undergoing repair it is to be utilised as commercial outlets. Built in 1545, the upper part of the building was used as a treasury and the lower part as a bakery of the Order, and was known to the people of Birgu as 'the rich men's oven'. The head of the Auberge de Provence was in charge of operations. When the Order moved into Valletta the building was converted into a store.

The next building is the Carmelite Church (with a main entrance in St Lawrence Street) built in 1611. The Church and Convent are no longer in use.

Next, we come to an impressive Baroque Palazzo sometimes known as Scamp's Palace now used by the *Casino di Venezia* where you can have a flutter if you are so inclined (your passport or ID Card are needed on your first visit). The restaurant serves good food and there is a lovely view of the Grand Harbour.

A five-star hotel is proposed on the empty site adjoining the gaming rooms. Originally, a palace stood here which was used by the Lieutenant General of the Galleys who was the Superintendent of the Order's Arsenal. The palace was totally destroyed in an air raid during the war.

Also destroyed is the next building formerly the Palace of the Captains of the Galley Squadrons. Its neighbour – the Palace of the Captain of the Galleys was badly damaged but some of it survived the ravages of war.

The Caraffa Stores come next, recently restored and used as a centre for exhibitions and cultural events. They were built in 1689 by the Italian Grand Master Gregorio Caraffa (1680-1690) who encouraged trade and industry. They were used for storage or officers quarters.

Nearby is the famous castle of St Angelo, the upper part of which has been leased to the Sovereign Military Order of Malta, so that in a way the knights have come back, at least to a small but important part of Malta which they ruled from 1530 to 1798.

Other parts of the fortress are undergoing repair and restoration.

Dungeons for Galley-Slaves

The dungeons in which galley-slaves were kept, during the few hours when they were off duty, are situated under the Palace of the General of the Galleys on the waterfront. Though remnants remain, the dungeons, known as *Guvi* have been destroyed.

A Frenchman Jean Martelle de Bergerac, who was himself condemned to serve in the galleys in 1701, left behind a graphic picture of the ghastly existence of the Galley-slaves. He wrote:

> *'They are chained six to a bench. The benches are four feet wide, covered with sacking stuffed with wool. The officer who is master of the galley-slaves remains aft with the Captain to receive his orders; there are two under-officers, one amidships and one at the prow; all of these are armed with whips with which they flog the absolutely naked bodies of the slaves. Sometimes the galley-slaves row ten, twelve and even twenty hours at a stretch and on these*

16. The Monument to Grand Master Nicolas Cotoner (1663-1680) in the Valletta Cathedral. Cotoner was responsible for the massive defences known as the Cottonera Lines

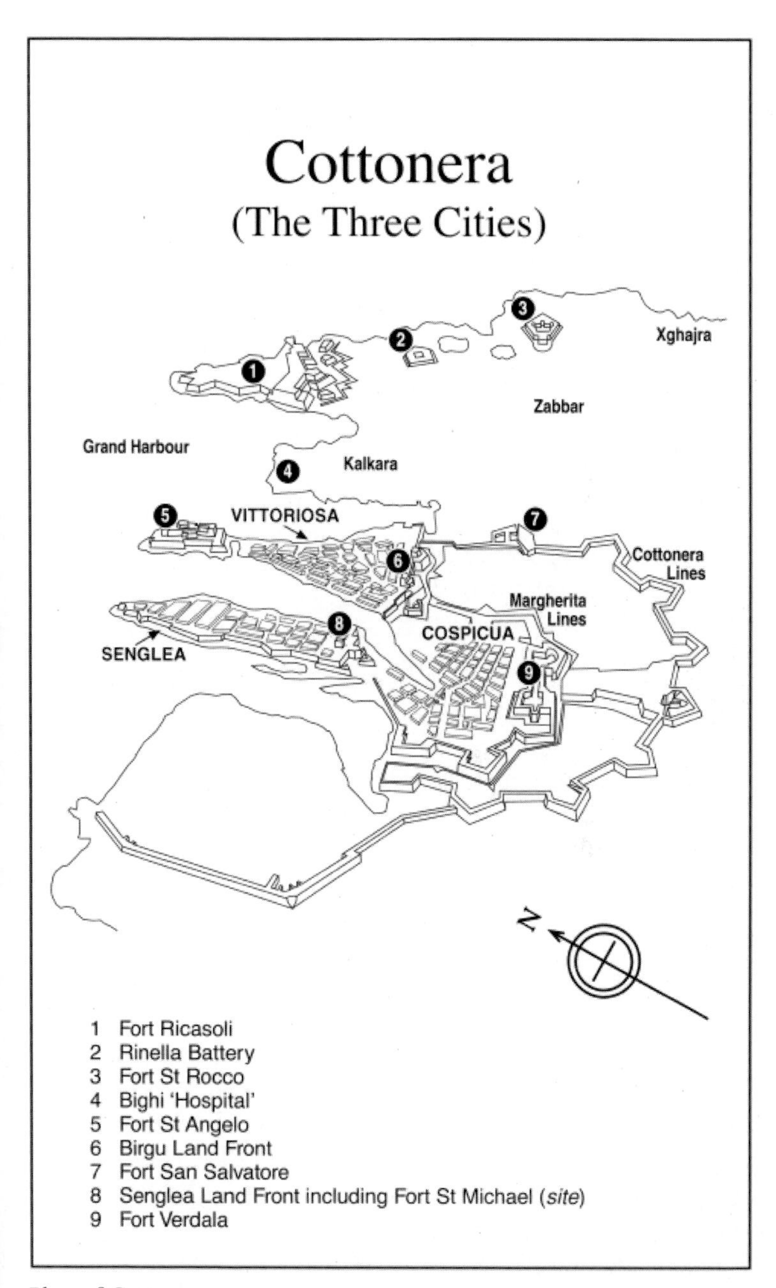

Plan of Cottonera

occasions the officer will go round putting into the mouth of the wretched rowers pieces of bread soaked in wine to prevent them from fainting. Then the Captain will call upon the officers to redouble their blows, and if one of the slaves fall fainting upon the oar, which is a common occurrence, he is flogged until he appears dead and then flung overboard without ceremony.'

La Valette in his younger days had spent a year at the oars having been captured when he lost his ship the *San Giovanni* in a skirmish at sea in 1541. An exchange of prisoners between the two antagonists saved him from further pain and possibly death.

The Maritime Museum
(Vittoriosa map reference 20)

City gate, Valletta Bus Terminus, Cospicua Bus No. 1 and 2. Opening hours: 9a.m. to 5p.m. (Telephone 21660052.) Entrance fee.

Formerly a British Naval Bakery, providing bread and biscuits for the Royal Navy and designed by architect William Scamp, this building now houses the Maritime Museum in Vittoriosa, opened in 1992. During the time of the Order this site was taken by the Galley Arsenal busily engaged in shipbuilding and ship-repairing.

The Museum displays a good collection of model ships and other items illustrating the long history of the island and its connections with navies of the various powers holding sway in the Mediterranean with Malta as their base. For nearly two hundred years, Malta was the home for the British Mediterranean Fleet. In the Hall is the splendid figurehead of H.M.S. Hibernia which was the flagship of the naval station for over fifty years.

The Maltese have been sea-farers for many centuries: they manned several of the galleys of the Knights when involved in commercial or war-like activities against corsairs and the Ottoman navy. More recently, hundreds of Maltese served on British naval and mercant vessels throughout the world, and were active during the war of the Crimea and of the First and the Second World Wars.

Over the main staircase are two large painting representing Malta and Britain by artist Ramiro Calì exhibited at the Malta Pavilion at the British Empire Exhibition held in London in 1924. One room is dedicated to traditional Maltese sea craft.

Carmelite Church

A part of the church dedicated to Our Lady of Mount Carmel, re-built after World War II stands between the *Casino di Venezia* (Scamp's Palace) and the Maritime Museum. What remains of the older part is in the street of St Lawrence. The Church and Convent were built in 1611 by the Carmelite Friars who first arrived in Malta in 1370, and established a Convent on the outskirts of Rabat.

In 1886 the Convent in Vittoriosa was handed over to the Franciscan Sisters who ran a school for small children. Neither Church nor Convent are now in use.

Casino di Venezia **(Scamp's Palace)**
(Vittoriosa map reference 23)

The Captain General of the Order of St John had his residence in this palace on the waterfront, often referred to as Scamp's Palace. It is now used as a Gaming Casino – *The Casino di Venezia*. The owners plan to build a five-star hotel next to the Casino'.

William Scamp was a British architect and engineer who came to Malta in 1841. He was responsible for St Paul's Anglican Pro-Cathedral in Valletta, the Naval

Scamp's Palace

Bakery – capable of supplying 30,000 lbs of bread and biscuits to a day working round the clock – as well as the drydock in Dockyard Creek. *(The Bakery is now the Maritime Museum,* *see page* 66*)*

The first stone for the dry dock was laid in 1844 and the yard opened in 1848 – this was the first dry dock for the Royal Navy on an overseas station. Scamp visited Malta on several other occasions and set up his office and stores in the former Palace of the General of the Galleys on the Birgu waterfront, to which he made some alterations – hence the name, Scamp Palace.

Caraffa Stores

Recently restored, the Caraffa Stores were built in 1689 during the reign of Grand Master Gregorio Caraffa (1680–1690), an Italian knight, and a keen promoter of commerce. It was during his reign that an alliance against the Turks was formed; the principle members being the Pope, the Republic of Venice, the Emperor Leopold, the King of Poland and the Knights of St John. The Alliance lasted for several years and many expeditions against Turkish territory were undertaken. Most of these were successful. But a defeat was suffered at Negro Ponte where an army of Maltese soldiers headed by thirty-nine Knights was exterminated. In 1688, an English fleet under the command of the Duke of Grafton visited the island, and was warmly received by the Grand Master who probably hoped that King James would re-establish the valuable Priories of England which had been abolished by Henry VIII.

The Caraffa Stores served as private quarter for two captains of the Order's larger sea vessels, and as a warehouse. The stores were built on three levels.

Early in the 19th century the Stores provided accommodation for British Army officers, and in 1818 the building was handed over to the Royal Navy. It is estimated that the stores on the Vittoriosa waterfront were capable to holding six months supply of food for 10,000 men, and the building was then known as Captain' Stores.

After restoration by the Cottonera Waterfront Group, the building has been used as an operational base for the Rolex Middle Sea Race and for the holding of Exhibitions. Included among these was one devoted to works by Caravaggio who had sought refuge in Malta following a dual in Rome in which a man was killed. He painted the *Beheading of St John* and *St Jerome* (both in the Valletta Co-Cathedral), got into hot water once again and fled from his prison cell in the Castle of St Angelo.

He died in Rome in 1610.

Fort St Angelo
(Vittoriosa map reference 27)

The lower part of St Angelo is usually open from June to September, on Saturday from 10 a.m to 1 p.m.; October to May, Saturday 10 a.m. to 2 p.m. (entrance fee covers a visit to St Elmo in Valletta). One way to get to the Castle is by boat from Customs House steps in Valletta; alternatively from Vittoriosa Wharf, bus no 1 and 2.

Proudly in command of the great harbour, the castle of St Angelo is the most famous and oldest fort in the Maltese Islands. Its history is the history of Malta, and it was here that a Phoenician, and later a Roman temple were built. Strengthened by the Arabs, the Normans, the Spaniards and the British, St Angelo was the headquarters of the Order of St John from 1530 until 1575 and was the bedrock of knightly defence in the Great Siege of 1565. It also played a prominent part during World War II.

Soon after 1576, the Castle was used as the state prison of the Order and in 1581, the Knights kept the Grand Master, Jean de la Cassiere prisoner there. He was accused

Fort St Angelo

of favouring members of his own Langue, neglecting the defences of the island, and of immorality. Summoned to Rome by the Pope he pleaded his case and as a result, his detractors were ordered to make public submissions to de la Cassiere who, however died before he could return to Malta.

After the fall of Fort St Elmo in Valletta, the Turkish commander looked at St Angelo across the harbour and is said to have exclaimed "If so small a son cost us so dear, what price shall we pay for so mighty a father".

The Castle was garrisoned by the British Army for a hundred years and served as headquarters of the

St Angelo from Valletta

Royal Navy from 1903. It remained so until the withdrawal of the British forces from Malta in 1979, and its distinguished commanders included Lord Louis Mountbatten.

The Allied invasion of Sicily was planned from St Angelo. On September 11, 1943, Admiral of the Fleet, Sir Andrew Cunningham signalled the British Admiralty: 'Be pleased to inform Their Lordships that the Italian Fleet is now anchored under the guns of Malta.'

St Angelo had two ancient chapels – one built around 1090 by Roger the Norman and dedicated to the Blessed Virgin (totally destroyed during the War) and the second dedicated to St Anne, first built by the De Nava family in the fifteenth century and rebuilt in 1831. It was then known as the *Castello a Mare* – the Castle-by-the-Sea.

The fort underwent various changes: in 1689 defence works were added by the military engineer Grunenburgh and the fort given the outline that survives today. Grunenburgh's Coat of Arms appears on the Main Gate on the Birgu quay.

The British added further structures in the nineteenth century. After 1912, the Fort served as a shore establishment of the Royal Navy and it was officially listed as a ship, first under the name of His Majesty's Ship (H.M.S.) Egmont and, in 1933 it was renamed H.M.S. St Angelo. It suffered extensively during the war and

Malta's connection with the Royal Navy dates back to 1674. Knight Charles I of England wrote to Grand Master Nicholas Cotoner whom he referred to as 'our cousin and friend', informing him that pirates from the Barbary coast had obliged him to keep a naval squadron permanently in the Mediterranean and asking 'his most eminent Prince' for facilities to purchase slave crews and provisions. A year later, a squadron under the command of Admiral Sir John Narborough called at Malta.

Chapel of St Anne at St Angelo

received some seventy direct hits during aerial bombardment.

Several British officials and their wives claim to have seen the 'Grey Lady' said to haunt the castle and to have done so since the Middle Ages. The Lady is friendly, and wears a long dress and a sort of pointed headdress. She is beautiful and sad and is said to have been the loved one of

the last Aragonese Governor of the Fort, a member of the di Nava family. She died, so they say, accidentally, under mysterious circumstances.

Extensive restoration works have been carried out and part of the old Castle has been leased to the Order of St John, so that the flag of the Order flies once again over a small part of the Maltese islands.

The ground floor of St Angelo is undergoing repair and restoration – who knows if the 'Grey Lady' will make an appearance?

The Parish Church of St Lawrence *(Map reference 18)*
City Gate, Terminus in Valletta. Cospicua Bus no. 1. Alight at Bus Terminus and enter Vittoriosa.

People in Vittoriosa claim that their Parish Church of St Lawrence was founded at the same time – 1090 – as the Cathedral in Mdina, the island's old Capital City. Be that as it may, there has certainly been a church next to the waterfront in Vittoriosa from ancient times. It has undergone alterations over the centuries. Originally known as *San Lorenzo a Mare* it was the first Conventual Church of the Order of St John having been taken over by the knights on their arrival in 1530, and having witnessed colourful events of the aristocratic Order, such as the investment of the first seven Grand Masters, and the

> When ordered to hand over the church valuables, prior to being put to death in the year 258, Lawrence assembled the poor and sick and presented them to the Prefect in Rome: 'Here', he said, 'is the church's treasure'. He was put to death by being roasted on a grid. From the fourth century onwards he was venerated as one of the most famous martyrs of the city of Rome. His emblem is a gridiron.

Parish Church of St Lawrence

solemn service of thanksgiving on the successful conclusion of the Great Siege in 1565.

Two years after being taken over by the knights, a fire broke out destroying much of the Church and many of its treasures, including a set of tapestries brought over from Rhodes. The Church was rebuilt, probably as the fourth to be built on the site. The present baroque building dates back to 1681, with the famous Lorenzo Gafa' (1639–1703), a native of Birgu, as the architect.

The foundation stone was laid by Mgr Michael Molina, Bishop of Malta and part of the church opened to the public on the feast of St Lawrence in 1697. This coincided with the entry into Vittoriosa of the newly elected Grand Master, Raymond Perellos y Roccaful, a Spaniard, (1697-1720). The Church was badly damaged by a fire in 1532 and again during the Second World War.

It was here that Grand Master Fra Philippe Villiers de L'Isle Adam gave thanks on arriving in Malta on the 26th October 1530 for having found a safe haven after seven years wandering following the expulsion of his Order by the Turks from the island of Rhodes.

The Church of St Lawrence includes several paintings of note including *The Three Saints of The Plague (Paul, Roque and Sebastian)*, a work by Filippo Paladini (1544–1616), in the chapel of St Catherine of Alexandria. The painting may have been commissioned to mark the end of a great plague which devastated the island in 1592. Also in this Chapel is *The Mystic Marriage of St Catherine of Alexandria*, a copy by an anonymous artist after the original by Annibale Carraci (1540–1609).

Worthy of note is the altarpiece *The Martyrdom of St Lawrence* by Mattia Preti (1613–1699) which is held to be the largest canvas painted by the Italian master. King Louis XIV of France is said to have coveted the painting and expressed the wish to have it sent to him. This request was opposed by the clergy of St Lawrence who thought up a number of excuses to frustrate the King's wishes.

The titular statue of St Lawrence (martyred by the Roman Emperor Valerian in the year 258) is the work of an unknown artist: the statue's head and hands are made of wood and were brought over from Spain. The statue is dressed in rich vestments, following the Spanish tradition. The Dowager Queen Adelaide (widow of William IV of England) convalescing in Malta for some months, was shown round the island in December 1838, asked her retinue to stop to watch the procession which included the statue of St Lawrence being taken into the Parish Church.

The statue was taken to St Peter's Benedictine Nunnery in Mdina for safe keeping during World War II. It narrowly escaped damage when a bomb hit the convent during a night raid in 1942 killing two of the nuns. The Saint's statue returned to Vittoriosa in 1944 and the Feast of St Lawrence is celebrated with great pomp in this ancient city on the 10th August each year (*see page 151 for opening hours*).

Its treasury contains relics of the Order's days in Rhodes. These include the silver cross on which each successive Grand Master took the Oath of Fealty on the occasion of his election. From the date of the arrival of the Order in 1530 until the election of Grand Master del Monte in 1568 the newly elected Master took the oath of office in the church of St Lawrence.

Like many other ancient buildings, the Church of St Lawrence suffered heavily during the war and lost many of its treasures.

Among those buried in the Church of St Lawrence is Sir Nicholas Upton, Turcopilar and Governor of Birgu, who died fighting in 1551 during an incursion into Malta by a Turkish force led by the Turkish General Sinan Pasha, known in the West as Dragut. Dragut was himself killed in Malta during the siege of 1565.

Church Museum

The Collegiate Hall and the Museum are annexed to the Church of St Lawrence. Although many treasures were lost during the war several remain and these include the silver cross on which the Grand Masters took their oath during investiture; intricate church vestments; silver antipendiums and others. This Museum is however rarely opened to the public.

Oratory of St Joseph (Museum)

A Church Museum, run by volunteers, is situated just off the main square – Victory Square – and this contains many items of interest including the sword and hat worn by the leader of the Knights during the Great Siege of 1565 – Grand Master Jean Parisot de la Valette. But the jewelled sword given by Philip II of Spain to the Grand Master remains in the Louvre, Paris, having been taken there by Napoleon. The Museum is open each morning between 9.30am and 12.30pm.

When the Knights came to Malta they brought with them a beautiful and precious icon of our Lady of Damascus (now in the Greek Catholic Church in Valletta). This was first placed in what was then the Church of St Catherine, forming part of the Oratory of St Joseph. The icon has been described 'a thing of great beauty and historic importance in addition to being an expression of faith.'

Cardinal's House

Not far from the Oratory of St John, in St George's Street, is the house lived in by a Maltese prelate of distinction, Cardinal Sceberras Testaferrata (1678-1763), the only native of Malta to receive the red hat.

A relative of the Cardinal is likewise said to have lived in this house. She was Elizabeth Testaferrata Dorell. Married to the Marchese Dorell, a Frenchman of the *ancien regime*, she was a colourful character, moving freely in international circles of elegance and intrigue. She became Lady-in-Waiting to Caroline, wife of King Ferdinand of Naples, but the Queen is said to have become jealous of her and Bettina was forced to return to Malta. Lady Bettina welcomed Napoleon's invasion and entertained the French Emperor at her Villa in the village of Gudja (still there to this day). She later became disillusioned with the French and placed her Villa at the disposal of Colonel Thomas Graham (later General Lord Lynedoch) who commandd the Anglo-Maltese forces opposing Napoleon. Graham set up his headquarters in Bettina's residence.

Later, Graham was to entertain Nelson and Emma Hamilton in Gudja when Nelson's flagship the *Foudroyant* visited Malta in May 1800.

1565 Museum

(follow the signposts form the Main Gate. Entrance fee)

Not far from the Main Gate is a small Museum devoted to the Great Siege of 1565 in which Birgu played an important part and was given the name of Vittoriosa – the Victorious One – (telephone 21891365)

Executioner's House

The Executioner's House in Pope Alexander VII Street, corner with Pacifico Scicluna Street. This official lived here, free of charge in return from carrying out his gruesome duties. Notice the 'two axes' carved in stone on top of one of the windows.

There is also an attractive 'Norman' window in a house in North Street, which is said to have been built during the 13/14th century. Similar windows are to be found in Notabile (Mdina), the medieval Capital City.

Palace of the Inquisitor

(Museum, map reference 15)

City Gate Bus Terminus in Valletta. Cospicua Bus No. 1. Opening hours: 9a.m. to 5p.m. (closed on Public Holidays); (telephone 21663731, Curator); (telephone 21827006 Museum Officer); (Entrance fee)

The Inquisitor's Palace is a vast 16th century building in Main Gate Street, *(Triq il-Mina l-Kbira)* built to design by the resident engineer of the Order of St John, Nicolo' Flavari. It has survived the ravages of time, revolution and the blitz of World War II, and is one of a few remaining palaces of its kind once found all over Europe. It was first built as the law courts of the Order of St John soon after the arrival of the Knights in 1530.

The Inquisitor's Palace (*interior*)

The first Inquisitor, Mgr Pietro Dusina, arrived in 1574 when the Grand Master, Jean l'Eveque de la Cassiere, a Frenchman, asked the Pope to help settle a dispute which had arisen between him and the Bishop. Architect Leonard Mahoney wrote about this building: *'if clarity, balance and gravity are the main characteristics of the Roman High Renaissance, then the Inquisitor's Palace may lay claim to be the nearest Maltese composition to satisfy the standards set by this golden age.'*

The Inquisition of Holy Office, as it was known, acted as a watchdog against heresy and enjoyed jurisdiction over all in the Maltese islands. The Inquisitor was a man of importance and there were sixty-two who resided at the Palace. Twenty-two subsequently became Cardinals and two became Popes, as Alexander VII (1655-67) and Innocent XII (1691-1700). Although not as severe as the Spanish Inquisition – most sentences for first offenders were of a spiritual nature, including fasting and prayer, but those charges could face imprisonment, (the Palace includes prison cells), beatings, rowing in the galleys or exile. Torture was used, only rarely and could not last more than thirty minutes. Blasphemy, apostasy to Islam during periods of slavery, bigamy and belief in magic all received attention from the Inquisitor and his servants. Those found guilty were handed over to the secular arm.

The Inquisitor Fabio Chigi (who later became Pope Alexander VII), wrote in one of his despatches about a Grand Mater who had a reputation for luxury and self-indulgence - he once entertained 600 guests to dinner at his Palace in San Anton.

The Inquisitor did not mince his words: "The Grand Master (Antoine de Paul, 1623-1636) is dying but without altering his irreverence, his sensuality, his duplicity, his selling favours, his twisting justice after his own fashion, his saying that 'briefs and citations are priests' stock-in trade and his indifference to censure..."

But however benign the Roman Inquisition was claimed to be when compared with the Spanish Inquisition, the torture inflicted could nonetheless be excruciating. That most commonly used was the *strappado*. The hands of the accused would be tied behind his back, and by a rope attached to a pulley in the ceiling, the accused would be pulled up so that the arms and shoulders supported the weight of his body. On occasions, heavy weights were attached to his feet to increase pressure and pain on his arms. The use of torture was finally banned in 1816.

During the French occupation the commander of the Cottonera district made use of the Inquisitor's palace. Napoleon abolished the inquisition following the conquest of Malta by the French in 1798. The British at first used the building as a military hospital and later as an Officers Mess. The Dominican monks whose church and priory were destroyed during the World War II used the Palace until they re-built their convent.

It is now a Museum.

Summer Palace

The Grand Inquisitor could probably relax in his Summer Palace, at Girgenti, Limits of Rabat. The attractive country house was built in 1625 on land taken from a person found guilty of heresy! Attached to it is a chapel dedicated to St Charles Borromeo, built in 1760 by Mgr Angelo Durini, another inquisitor. It is now used on occasions as a Malta's 'Chequers', by the Prime Minister of the day.

It had been kept in readiness for possible use by President George Bush (Snr), of the United States, and President Gorbachev of Russia during the Summit in Malta in December 1989. The meeting was successful, but the rough weather did not help and the two superpowers found it difficult to visit each others warships berthed, for reasons of security in Marsaxlokk harbour.

Dominican Church of the Annuncation
(Vittoriosa map reference 17)

The Dominicans arrived in Vittoriosa in 1527 and the monks built themselves a church – the Church of the Annunciation – and a convent, in what is now Main Gate Street. Most Inquisitors belonged to the Dominican Order and the Inquisitors donated many treasures to the Church including the High Altar. The church was popular and was much frequented by the crews of the galleys which berthed in the nearby Marina. It was badly damaged during the war but was rebuilt. The feast of St Dominic is celebrated at the end of August (*see page 152*).

An Unusual Dominican

There is an unusual story about a Vicar-General of the Dominican Order who died in Senglea. He was born a Turk and was captured when two years old and taken to Malta with his mother.

The background to this colourful event is that in 1664 Maltese galleys were cruising in the Dodecanese and were involved in a battle with a Turkish galleon the *Sultana*. Following a fierce battle the *Sultana* was captured. Aboard was a woman seemingly of importance, Zafire' by name together with her son, Osman. It was assumed that Zafire' was a favourite to the Sultan judging by the splendour of her wardrobe. Mother and son were taken to Malta where the Mother died soon after arrival. The son became the object of great interest among the knights. He turned Christian, joined the Dominican Order and was sent to Rome to train for the priesthood. He was known as Padre Ottoman. He returned to Malta after six years of study and became Vicar General of the Dominican Order of monks. He died in a small house in Senglea, aged thirty-four, a victim of the plague. This particular epidemic ravaged the island for nine months between 1675 and 1676 and carried off some 11,000 of the inhabitants.

The Clock Tower in Victory Square

'There was once an old clock-tower
In the centre of the square,
And for those of us who knew it
It has never moved from there.'

L.A. BUTTIGIEG

In Victory Square *(Misraħ ir-Rebħa)* in the centre of the City stood a Clock Tower which was a landmark – the square was known as *Piazza dell'Orologio*. Along with many other historical monuments it was destroyed during the war.

Hopefully, the Tower from which Grand Master la Valette kept an eye on things during the Great Siege, and the bells in the Tower, (manufactured in Messina in 1504 and used to sound the alarm in times of danger) will be rebuilt – the clock works have been preserved. The matter is under discussion.

This famous Tower was built in 1549, although some claim it is older, and the clock installed in 1629. It was destroyed in an air raid on the 4th of April 1942.

Also in the main square is a statue of St Lawrence, patron of the City, erected in 1880, and the Victory Monument dating back to 1705 which depicts Malta in battle armour. Also in this square is a stone crucifix a reminder of the executions carried out here in the 16th century.

Among those executed in this square was Giuseppe Callus, a Maltese doctor of medicine and a patriot, courageous enough to protest against the Order's high handed behaviour in trampling on the privileges of the Maltese, which the Knights had sworn to uphold. He was

Victory Monument in Victory Square, Birgu

executed on order of Grand Master La Valette: the knights, under constant threat of invasion, did not tolerate opposition or dissidents.

When George VI visited Malta and the Three Cites in 1943, he stopped in Victory Square to look at the heavy damage. He was accompanied by the Parish Priest and was given a warm welcome by the people.

It was George VI who awarded the George Cross to

Malta in April 1942, 'to bear witness to a heroism and devotion to duty that will long famous in history.'

Winston Churchill also visited the Dockyard in 1943.

Situated in the square is a Band Club where you can relax and have a drink.

The Auberges

Auberge of England

(see map of Vittoriosa reference 5)

When the Order of St John arrived in Malta in 1530 they soon got down to business. They set about building a Magisterial palace and, of course, a Hospital since apart from being warriors, they were established by Pope Pascal II in 1113 to look after pilgrims to the Holy Land.

Priority was also given to the construction of Auberges (or Inns) to house the various nationalities making up the Order of Chivalry. A few of these Auberges survive to this day; others have disappeared, several of them having been destroyed during World War II. When moving to their new Capital, Valletta, the Knights constructed new premises larger and more comfortable than those which they inhabited in Vittoriosa.

Of the original Auberges the Auberge of England in 39-40 Mistral Street, survives and has been converted into a library.

Sir Clement West acquired the premises in 1534 for the English Knights, although the first English Knight to set foot in Malta was probably Fra Nicholas Hussey who formed part of the mission to Malta in 1526 sent to report to the Grand Master on the suitability of otherwise of the island. The report was not enthusiastic but the Knights having wandered for seven years without success had little choice.

Henry VIII who later seized all the possession of the

Auberge d'Angleterre

Order in England, was among the first to congratulate the Order on its safe arrival. It was also King Henry who had been given the honorary title of *fides defendor*, 'Defender of the Faith', for his learned treatise published in 1521 in which he refuted what he then saw as heresies of Martin Luther. It is for this reason that *'F.D.'* appeared round the British Sovereign's head in British coins.

Grand Master L'Isle Adam visited Henry VII in London in 1521 seeking support for an attempt to recapture the island of Rhodes from which the Knights had been expelled. The King of England gave the Grand Master a gift of nineteen cannons some of which were used in the defence of Tripoli which eventually fell to the Turks in 1551.

A few English Knights continued to work in the interests of the Order despite Henry VIII. One of them, Sir Nicholas Upton, lost his life in the Great Siege of 1565 and is buried in the Church of St Lawrence. During the siege, the English Langue was responsible for the defence of that stretch of bastion from the Holy Infirmary to Fort St Angelo. At their head was Sir Oliver Starkey who was the Grand Master's Latin Secretary. When the relief force arrived from Sicily and the Turkish forces withdrew there were two English Knights, of the Order, Fra John Smith and Fra Edward Stanley. Since the English Knights were unable to have their own Auberge in Valletta when the Order moved there in 1572 the Auberge in Vittoriosa is the only one of its kind in Malta.

During the last few days of the Order in Malta, in 1783 the title of the dormant Langue of England became, with the consent of King George III, a part of the designation of a new Langue set up by the Elector of Bavaria and Grand Master de Rohan. To this Langue was allotted as its 'Inn' the Palace commonly known as the 'Baviere', near St Elmo in Valletta.

Next to the Auberge of England in Vittoriosa is the residence of Sir Oliver Starkey, one of the few English knights in Malta after the suppression of the English Langue by Henry VIII. He was the Latin Secretary to La Valette and wrote the inscription on the Grand Master's tomb in St John's Co-Cathedral in Valletta, which reads (in translation):

> *Here lies La Valette, worthy of eternal honour, he who was formerly the terror of Asia and Africa and the shield of Europe, whence by his holy arms he expelled the barbarians, the first to be buried in this beloved city of which he was the founder.*

Auberge de France
(24-27 Hilda Tabone Street, Vittoriosa map reference 8)

The Auberge de France together with those of Auvergne and of Provence formed an important part of the Order of St John – all built in an area 'reserved' for the Knights and known as the *Collachio*. The Auberge de France was one of the first to be completed in Vittoriosa and continued to be used even after the French built more imposing premises in Valletta. The French were assigned the duty of supervising the *Sacra Infermeria* (the 'Hospital') and the Knight in charge was known as a Pilier of the Order. Following the opening of the Auberge in Valletta the Inn in Vittoriosa was neglected, and in 1830 was used as a primary school and later as a carpenter's shop. It was purchased from private hands by the Government of the day in 1938. Post-war it was used for a short while as a Museum of Political History and was closed in 1987. The plan at the moment is to turn this building into a Museum dealing with the social history of the Maltese language.

The French played a prominent part of the history of the Order. Eleven of their Knights became Grand Masters in Malta, and these included L'Isle Adam, Alof de Wignacourt and Jean Parisot de la Valette, hero of the Great Siege. Relations between Malta and France were

Auberge de France

often close, and French spoken by many. The daughters of King Louis XV rented a garden in Malta, and the Grand Masters, playing a game of diplomacy would sent Maltese oranges to Monarchs and other prominent personalities in the capitals of Europe. A portrait by Antoine Favray of Grand Master de Rohan at the Museum of Fine Arts in Valletta includes a prominent orange tree in the left hand corner of the painting.

The Auberge de France in Valletta was destroyed during one of the three thousand or so air raids in World War II, and the site was then utilised as headquarters of the General Workers Union. The Auberge in Vittoriosa is therefore the only remainder of the French Knights.

What remains of other Auberges in Vittoriosa can be traced in the area of the *Collachio* – the Auberges of Auvergne and Provence; Germany, in Victory Street, Castille and Portugal, as well as Aragon also in Hilda Tabone Street. The exception was the Auberge of Italy, which was to be found in St Lawrence Street near the waterfront since the duties of the Italian Langue included naval and maritime matters. The grandiose Auberge d'Italie in Valletta is in Merchant Street and is now used by the Ministry of Tourism.

Auberge d'Italie (site)
(St Lawrence Street, towards St Angelo, Vittoriosa map reference 20)

The Auberge d'Italie lies outside the *Collachio* and was built nearer the Castle of St Angelo (in the street of St Lawrence.) In days gone by the Italians also ran a small hospital dedicated to St Catherine. Since the post of Captain General of the Fleet was the responsibility of the Langue of Italy, it was felt necessary to have their 'Inn' nearer the sea because of their naval and maritime commitments.

The first carnival to be held in Birgu after the arrival of the Order is said to have been held here in 1535 and the festive days of Carnival are still held to this day. One Grand Master who tried to subdue the enthusiasm was given short shift by the people.

The Auberge was unfortunately among the many historical buildings demolished during the war years.

Architect Hugh Braun, a member of the commission reporting in 1944 on damage caused to the island's historic monuments had this to say of Birgu:

> *'This famous town, long ago stormed for four months by all the might of Islam, has now suffered a siege which has laid it once more in ruins, The Castle of St Angelo, citadel of the defence, yet stands, battered but still the residence of its captain; southwards stretches a ruin-field, unsurpassed for desolation in Malta. Churches, houses, even the streets have disappeared; it is impossible to discover the whereabouts of known monuments or make exploration for new discoveries'.*

Monastery of Santa Scolastica

(Formerly Hospital of the Order)
(Vittoriosa map reference 7, in St Scolastica Street)

One of the first tasks undertaken by the order of St John in this maritime city was the building of a hospital, *The Sacra Infermeria*. This was situated overlooking Kalkara Creek, and like all hospitals run by the Order, it quickly became famous throughout Europe.

Since the Order of St John kept the Turks at bay in the Mediterranean and gained renown for their military and naval skills, one tends to forget that the *raison d'etre* of the founders was the care of the sick and of the wounded. In Vittoriosa, as in other hospitals run by the knights, the physicians had to be 'learned and experienced' and the surgeons were to be 'prudent, discreet and skilful in their profession'. The hospital was enlarged in 1538, although this did not prove sufficient to deal with the numerous casualties during the four months of fierce fighting in the siege of 1565.

It was one of the first Hospitals in Europe to admit patients of different creeds. Food was served by Novices of the Order on silver plate and it is believed that the Knights introduced the practice in the seventeenth century of keeping surgical instruments in boiling water before use with the object of making operations less painful, and also maintaining a high level of hygiene.

When the Order moved to Valletta and built a new hospital, the building in the Vittoriosa was handed over to the cloistered Benedictine nuns of Santa Scolastica. The Nuns had previously had their convent in Mdina, the Capital, having been established there in 1494. They had utilised the site of a Jewish synagogue vacated when King Ferdinand and Queen Isabella of Spain expelled the Jewish community from their territory in 1492. The nuns moved to Vittoriosa in 1604 where they remain to this day. Among the valuable paintings taken to Birgu by the nuns from their Convent in Mdina is the *Retable of The Candlemas Madonna* by Girolamo Spagnuolo. The painting has the Virgin Mary in the centre panel with a lively Child Jesus on her lap. The side panels depict St Scolastica and St Benedict.

There is a small church attached to the Convent, dedicated to St Anne. It was built to a design of Lorenzo Gafa (1639–89), who was a son of Birgu and responsible for a number of splendid Baroque Churches in Malta.

The Jewish Community

Nearby is a street called the Street of the Jews, marking an area inhabited by the Jewish community who played an important part in Maltese life both in Birgu and in Mdina (the Capital city), having their own schools, doctors and hospitals and their own cemeteries (*see page 147*). There is also a 'Jews Sally Port' not far from the Monastery of St Scolastica in *Triq il-Mandraġġ* facing Kalkara Creek.

In 1492 King Ferdinand and Queen Isabella of Spain expelled the Jewish community from their Empire.

In the fifteenth century the Jewish community in Birgu was small but they had their own Synagogue. Another Synagogue was at Mdina where Jews were more numerous; it is estimated that between one fourth and one third of the population in the old Capital City was Jewish. At the time, the Jews were the only large non-Christian community in Malta since the Muslims had been expelled from the Island around the middle of the thirteenth century.

The Bishop's Palace
(Map Reference 13)

The Bishop's Palace is in Old Bishop's Palace Street, having been built there by Bishop Cubelles soon after the arrival in Malta of the Order of St John in 1530. Bishop Galiares enlarged it in 1515-33; he was the last Bishop to have his seat in Birgu. When the Order took up residence in Valletta the Grand Master did not favour having a Bishop's Palace in the new City, since he held this would 'cast a shadow on the jurisdiction of the Order'. The Bishop countered that his 'fold extended wherever his sheep might wander'. As often happened, the dispute ended up in Rome, and it was some time before the Bishop was allowed to move. Following arguments and counter-arguments, pleas and counter-pleas, the Bishop was allowed to build his Palace, but, in order to remind him of the limits of his authority, he was not allowed to build dungeons, as he had done elsewhere.

When granting Malta to the Order of St John, the Emperor Charles V stipulated that the nomination of Bishops was to be in hands of his Viceroy in Sicily. The Order was bound to submit three names one of which was

A quick-tempered Spaniard, Tommaso Gargallo by name, was Bishop of Malta for thirty-seven years (1578-1614), and was said 'to have tormented the reigns of three Grand Masters.' His relations with the Inquisitor were not much better. He took offence when one Inquisitor suspended him from his Episcopal duties, (for refusing to pay part of the revenue to the Inquisitor) and ordered a Notice to this effect to be placed on the door of the Cathedral of Mdina. Gargallo hurried to Malta from nearby Siciy, tore down the offending notice attacked the deacon and chaplain, who had nailed it to the door, and the Clerk who had read out the notice to the congregation. When the Canons declined to acknowledge him while under papal ban, he made some of them prisoners, and dragged them behind his horse-drawn carriage all the way to his palace dungeons in Vittoriosa. Not surprisingly, two of the Canons died and there followed a public uproar. Relatives of the unfortunate Canons were awarded compensation. Gargallo was hastily summond to Rome for an explanation and the Pope ordered him to undertake a pilgrimage to the shrine of Monserrat in Spain, and to erect a church (The Jesuit Church in Valletta) as a sign of repentance.

to be a subject of the Spanish Crown. As a result, the Knights often looked on the Bishop as an agent of the King of Spain, and the Grand Inquisitor as a spy of the Pope.

The Bishop's Palace in Vittoriosa, is now in private hands and not open to the public.

The Bishop nowadays resides in Mdina, the old Capital, and he has another *Palazzo* in Valletta.

Bishops have always played an important part in the affairs of Malta and in the lives of the people. Both the Bishop and the Inquisitor sought to extend their jurisdiction so that the Grand Master – supreme ruler on the country – had to contend with two rival and powerful authorities. Friction between the three was often bitter. This gave rise to some confusion, but, despite this, the Bishop and the Inquisitor often acted as champions of the people of Malta.

17. Statue of the Patron Saint in the middle of Victory Square, Vittoriosa, on the occasion of the Feast Day of Saint Lawrence

18. The Look-Out Post at Senglea Point known as the *Gladjola*

19. The statue of *Maria Bambina* originally a figurehead of a vessel which foundered in the Adriatic, dates back to 1610, and is venerated in Senglea

20. An 18th century engraving of Senglea

21. Blitz: The Oratory Chapel of St Philip's in Senglea, built by the Knights of Malta and destroyed during the last war

22. The splendid palaces on the Waterfront in Vittoriosa

23. An impressive photograph taken at the turn of the century of Grand Harbour and The Three Cities with H.M.S. Hibernia in Dockyard Creek

24. Grand Master de la Sengle (1533-1557) who gave his name to the walled city of Senglea

25. The Main Gate – St Helen – leading into Cospicua; and (*below*) the bastions of Senglea

26. The imposing Notre Dame Gate (also known as Zabbar Gate and Cotoner Gate)

27. The 100-ton gun at Fort Rinella, and (*below*) Bighi Naval Hospital built in 1863

28. An engraving by Charles Brockdorff of the Arsenal and of the *Macina* and (below) the *Capitana* of Grand Master de Rohan

29. Statue of the 'Risen Christ' which is carried 'at speed' during Easter

30. The Church of St Lawrence, Vittoriosa, on the occasion of the feast day of the Patron Saint, and (*below*) *The Martyrdom of St Lawrence* the Altarpiece by Mattia Preti

31. A painting by Filippo Paladini (c.1544-1616) depicting *The Three Saints of the Plague* (St Paul, St Roque, and St Sebastian) in the Church of St Lawrence

32. The 16th century Clock Tower which was a landmark in Victory Square, Birgu, and which was destroyed during World War II. There are plans to have it rebuilt

Senglea (*L-Isla*)

(see map on pages 114–115 Bus no.3)

Dockyard Creek (Galleys Port) separates Vittoriosa from Senglea *(L'Isla)*. Both Cities fought valiantly and suffered greatly during the Siege of 1565, and again in World War II, when all three Cities bore the brunt of repeated air attacks by the Luftwaffe. It is estimated that the seventy-five per cent of all buildings in Senglea were totally destroyed. Many, if not most of the inhabitants of some 4,000 are connected in one way or another with ships, shipbuilding and the dockyard.

Senglea owes its name, and its origin, to Grand Master Claude de la Sengle, a Frenchman (1553-1557).

The first Grand Master, Philippe Villieres de L'Isle Adam built himself a country house in the area, as did another Grand Master, Juan de Homedes, a Spaniard (1553-1557). Homedes was responsible for having built Fort St Michael (1552) which played a prominent part in the fighting of 1565, and which dominated the City. In recognition of the part is played during the Siege of 1565 it was given the name of *Civitas Invicata* (the Unconquered City). Fort St Michael was demolished in 1922 to make room for an elementary school and only part of its bastions remain today.

De la Sengle who proved himself wholly committed to embellishing the old City succeeded Homedes.

Senglea saw the birth of harbour boat races, which are still held today amid much enthusiasm and rivalry during the September 8th Regatta. The 8th of September was the day when the Great Siege of 1565 was finally lifted, and when Italy surrendered to Allied Forces in 1943. Both

Senglea

1 Mons Panzavecchia Street
2 Marina Street
3 4th September Square
4 Post of Italy
5 Fort St Michael (*site*)
6 Our Lady of Victories (Parish Church)
7 Residence of Cagliostro?
8 Garden of Grand Master d'Omedes (*site*)
9 St Philip Neri Church
10 Look-Out Post (*Gardjola*), Senglea Point
11 Drydock
12 Drydock
13 *Il-Macina*
14 Porto Salvo Sally Port

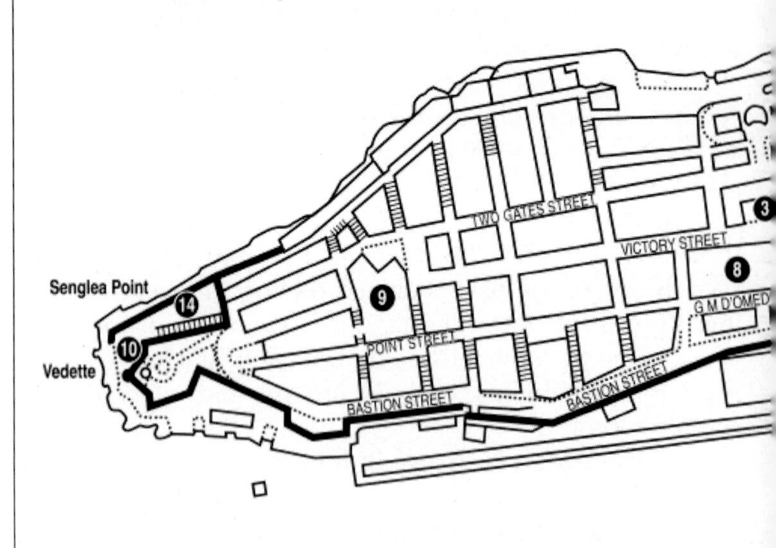

Plan of Senglea (*L-Isla*)

(Isla)

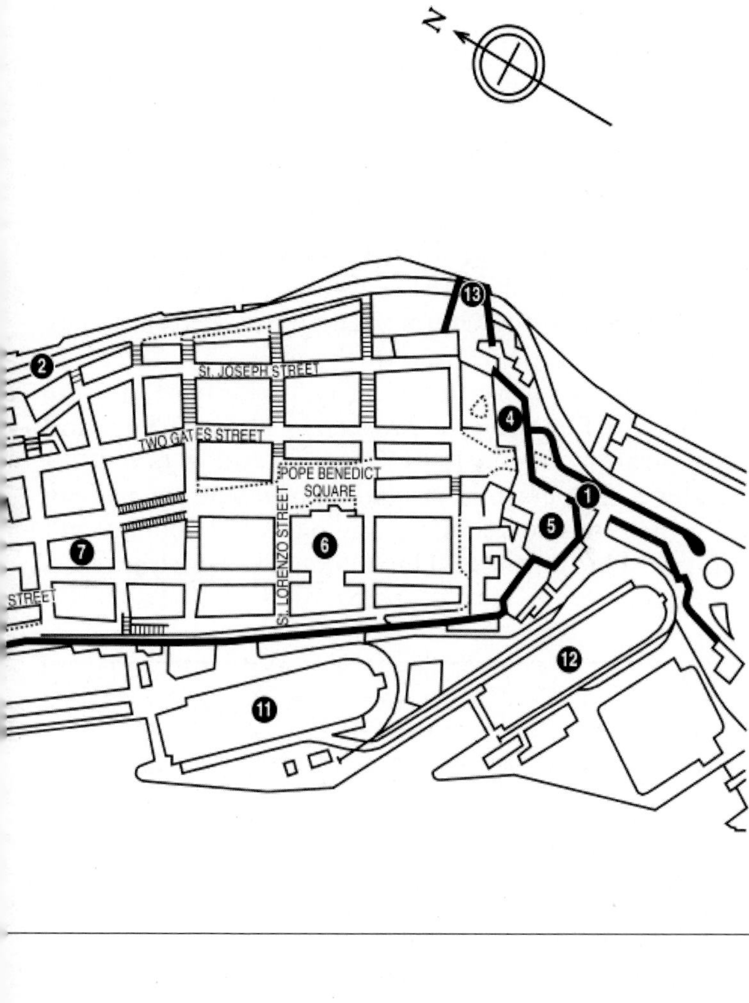

N

St. JOSEPH STREET
TWO GATES STREET
POPE BENEDICT SQUARE
St. LORENZO STREET
STREET

these events are also celebrated by the popular feast of the Nativity of our Lady, commonly known as *Il-Bambina*, an endearing and feminine version of *Il-Bambin* – the child Jesus.

Our Lady of Victories and other Churches *(Senglea map reference 6)*

The Church of Our Lady of Victories, in Pope Benedict's Square, was first built in 1743. It was destroyed in an air attack on the aircraft carrier H.M.S. Illustrious which was berthed in the nearby creek, but was rebuilt after the war.

In front of the church stands a monument honouring those who died during the war.

Another interesting church that of St Philip Neri, in Point Street, was built in 1612. Its altarpiece is by Stefano Erardi (1678) and the Oratory served as a Retreat House for priests and students from the Seminary.

Also much revered in Senglea is the feast and the statue of The Redeemer *(ir-Redentur)*. This is to be found in the Oratory of the Holy Crucifix and is taken out annually; a custom which started following a vow made in 1813 which had devastated many parts of Malta but not Senglea. The statue of The Redeemer which attracts

> Grand Master Francisco Ximenes de Texada (a Spaniard, 1773-1775) decided that the food supply should be increased by re-stocking the island with game and forbidding the shooting of rabbits. The Bishop complained that as rabbits destroyed crops their increase would provoke a famine. The Grand Master relaxed the law of the Episcopal lands, only to discover that the Bishop was using his concession to kill rabbits for himself and for his followers. Disputes of this kind were common and recourse was often made to the Pope who acted as a mediator.

Senglea Point

people from all over the islands also forms part of the Good Friday procession.

Another custom peculiar to Senglea takes place on the morning of Easter Sunday when a Statue of The Risen Christ is carried *at speed* through the streets of the town amid much clapping.

Not far from the Church of St Philip Neri is Senglea Point and the famous Vedette from where one gets a view of the Grand Harbour in all its majesty. Carved on the look-out post are a large ear, and an equally large eye,

The *Gladjola*

reminding the sentries to be very vigilant. There is a saying in Maltese which freely translated means, 'the air can see and the walls can hear'.

From here also you overlook *French Creek* and recall the saga of the aircraft carrier *Illustrious*.

On the Senglea quay facing Vittoriosa is a large bastion known as *il-Macina* where there used to be a large crane which lifted heavy objects from ships and galleys. *(see map of Senglea page 114–115)*

H.M.S. Illustrious

French Creek is where a new large drydock has been built. It was here, that the aircraft carrier H.M.S. Illustrious long a target of enemy aircraft, fought her fiercest battle for survival.

Four months after Mussolini declared war, Swordfish aircraft from H.M.S. Illustrious had crippled the Italian fleet at Taranto. Both the Germans and the Italians tried desperately to sink her in retaliation.

The 'Illustrious' joined Admiral Cunningham's Mediterranean Fleet in September 1940. While forming part of a convoy escort, Illustrious was dive bombed again and again by German stukas and was hit by six 1,000 lb. bombs. Badly listing to port but with her guns still firing defiantly, she arrived of Malta and was towed into Grand Harbour. The Nazi radio boasted that Malta's harbour would be the graveyard of the Illustrious.

On the 16th and 19th January 1941, renewed determined attacks by a hundred enemy aircraft were made on the Illustrious which was again hit. Much of Senglea was destroyed but thanks to the Island's anti-aircraft gunners and the skill of the Dockyard workers, H.M.S. Illustrious survived. On the 23rd January she slipped out to sea and reached Alexandria, and later to Norfolk, Virginia where she was completely reconditioned.

Prominent People

Various people who later became prominent were born in Senglea. These include three Bishops and Mgr Ignazio Panzavecchia, a prominent Churchman who was evidently the first choice to become Prime Minster under the 1921 Constitution. However, because of his priesthood he declined the offer, and Mr Joseph Howard was chosen in his stead. Entry into Senglea is through Mgr Panzavecchia Street (or through St Gaetan Gate). Another clergyman, born in Senglea who made a name for himself overseas was Dom Mauro Inguanez (see map for Square named after him). He was Librarian at the famous Monastery of Monte Cassino during the siege by the Germans during World War II, and managed to hide various treasures from them.

Also a native of Senglea was Juan Bautisto Azopardo (1772-1848) who rose to prominence in the navy of Argentina during the country's struggle for independence. There are several reminders in Buenos Aires of the part he played; and where he is something of a folk-hero. In Senglea a street on the waterfront is named after him and the Ambassador of Argentina, on a visit to Malta in 1990, unveiled a plague recording his birth (1772).

Another prominent person who made his name overseas, this time in Ontario, Canada was Louis Scickluna (1808-1871) who became a builder of ships. Also born in Senglea was Andrea De Bono (1821-1871) who traded in ivory in Africa, and who was one of the first to explore the White Nile.

Cagliostro's Residence *(map reference 7)*

'Count' Alessandro Cagliostro (real name Giuseppe Balsamo) is said to have had a house in what is now Victory Street *(Triq il-Vittorja)* in Senglea that was demolished during the last war. Cagliostro was a notorious impostor who claimed he was the illegitimate son of Grand Master Manoel Pinto de Fonseca, a Portuguese who reigned between 1741 and 1773. Among the many claims made by this charlatan was his boast of having concocted an elixir of life designed to keep man sound in health and strength. It is not known whether this worked, but the Grand Master did live to be ninety-two! The self styled 'Count' (born in Palermo, Sicily) had spent time in Bastille in Paris, was arrested in Rome and died in prison there in 1875.

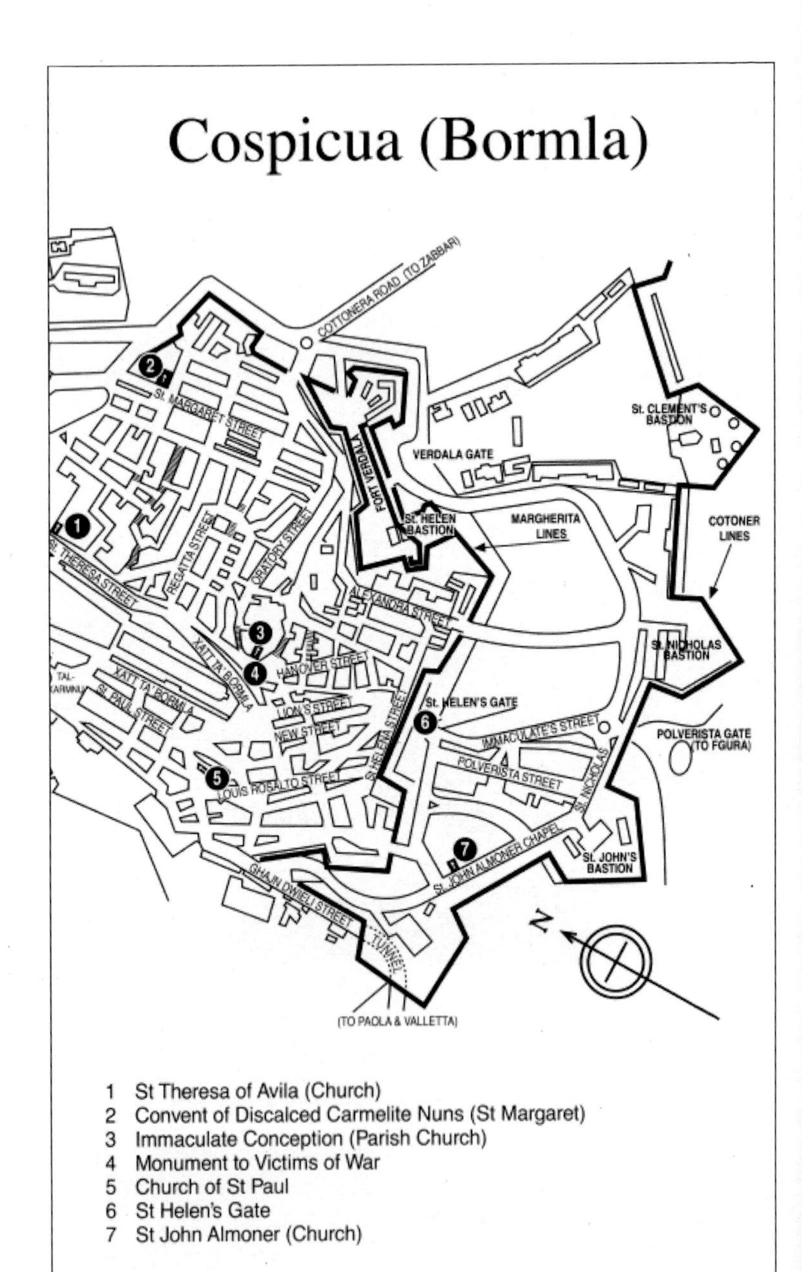

Plan of Cospicua

Cospicua *(Bormla)*

The largest and youngest of the Three Cities is Cospicua *(Bormla)*. Its shoreline is dominated by the Dockyard which has played a significant role in the history of the island. Like its neighbours it suffered greatly during the siege of 1565 as again during the World War II.

Church of the Immaculate Conception
(Cospicua map reference 3)

Its most significant treasure is the Collegiate Church of the Immaculate Conception. The first church to be built on the site dates back to 1584, and was dedicated to St John the Almoner. The church was enlarged in 1637 and again in later years until completed in 1732. It is an architectural gem. One of the most valuable works of art is an image of *Christ the Redeemer*, painted on copper.

The titular statue of the *Immaculate Conception* carved in wood is the work of Maria de Domenici, a Carmelite nun. The statue was covered in silver in 1905 – an event that did not gain universal praise. An object of much devotion is the *Crucifix of Candia*, brought to Malta from Crete in 1669 and of special interest is a set of statues used during the Good Friday procession.

One of the clocks on the façade of the Parish Church is by the Maltese clock-maker Michelangelo Sapiano. The Church has many treasures, including paintings by Antoine Favray and Giuseppe Calì. A chair dating back to the Order of St John is among the exhibits in the Church Museum.

Below the church and overlooking Santa Teresa street is the monument erected to the fallen in World War II.

Other Churches and Places of Interest

Other churches of interest include the Church and priory of St Teresa built in 1625 by the Order of Carmelites. Its convent served as a retreat house for the knights of the Order of St John. Successive Grand Masters would visit the church to be greeted by the Inquisitor before receiving the keys of Birgu.

Also in Cospicua is the Church of the Conversion of St Paul, built on the waterfront from where, according to some, Paul of Tarsus left after his three months visit. The present church was built in 1741, replacing the older one built in 1590.

Both the Margherita and the Cottonera Lines enclosed and defended Cospicua against invasion but these masterly works were never put to the test (*see page 38*)

There are eight gateways in the Cottonera Lines. The most imposing is the Zabbar Gate (*Notre Dame Gate, built in 1675*) and this leads to Zabbar; the Polverista Gate leads to Fgura, while the Salvatore Gate takes you to Kalkara.

Driving or walking alongside the Cottonera Lines one comes across the Polverista Gate, once used as a storage depot for gunpowder. In the vicinity is a chapel dedicated to St John the Almoner (1682) and Fort San Salvatore, also forming part of the Lines. It was used by the Turkish invaders who placed heavy guns to try to breach the Post of Castile, and they very nearly succeeded. This fort was built by grand Master Manoel de Vilhena in order to prevent a repetition. Fort San Salvatore is not open to the public.

Bir Mula Heritage House

Of unusual interest is the *Bir Mula Heritage House* in St Margaret Street. This is an old house which has undergone many alterations over the centuries and is now used as a permanent history and heritage exhibition. It is open on Saturday and Sunday from 10am to noon. (*Entrance fee*)(Telephone 21661000)

Shipbuilding and repairing have existed in Bormla since the Middle Ages. The coming of the Knights in 1530 widened and enlarged these facilities because of the Order's belief in having a powerful navy. In their turn, the British developed the Dockyard further and for many years this was the largest industry in the Maltese islands employing thousands of men. During the first World War (1914–18) the presence of four Allied navies in the Mediterranean – British, French, Italian and Japanese – all made demands on the docks where work was often carried out day and night, with nearly 16,000 men employed there.

The Dockyard

When the Order of St John came to Malta in 1530 they found a small dockyard which they soon enlarged, but the drydocks as we know them today date back to 1804. Continually enlarged by the British Admiralty there were seven docks just before the start of the war against Hitler. The first dock was opened in 1858.

In 1938, the number of ships comprising the British Mediterranean Fleet was around fifty and during the war years the number of dockyard workers, who did sterling work in repairing allied shipping, reached a total of 12,000. The dockyard, was of course, repeatedly attacked by Axis aircraft. (The Royal Navy relinquished the Dockyard in 1959).

Admiral Carden, C-in-C of the Allied Fleets drew the attention of the Lords of the Admiralty 'to the excellent work done by the Malta Dockyard'. In the course of a lecture, Rear-Admiral Ballard, Admiral Superintendent of the Yard said:

Cottonera Gate

'The First Lord informed me that war activity was at a higher pressure in Malta than in any other place outside the United Kingdom. Malta, he added, is a vital part of the line of communications, allied troopships and war vessels (800 per month) are passing through the island, numberless hospital ships carry thousands of sick and wounded thereto, allied merchant ships are working at high pressure day and night, and about 15,000 tons of coal are being handled each week.'

Fort San Salvatore built by the Order of St John in 1726 within the San Salvatore bastion forms part of the Cottonera Lines. It is not normally open to the public. (*see map of Cospicua*)

Also in Cospicua is St Edward's College which was once Cottonera Hospital built in 1837 and which played an important part during the Gallipoli and Salonika campaigns. It was founded by Lady Strickland in 1929 as a school for boys. Lady Strickland was the wife of Lord Strickland, (Prime Minister of Malta in 1927 to 1932), and a member of the wealthy Hulton family.

Prisoners of War

Attached to the Margherita Lines is another fort, Verdala, built by the British in 1853, to house British regiments. It is now a school. During the First World War the Fort together with the Barracks, St Clements Camp and the Polverista Barracks were used to intern hundreds of prisoners from Germany, Austria, Bulgaria, Turkey and Greece. Among these was Karl Doenitz, then a German naval officer serving aboard the submarine UB68 which was scuttled after being attacked by the Sloop *Snapdragon* in October 1918. At the end of the World War II, Doenitz, now a senior German Admiral was chosen by Hitler to succeed him.

One of many gates which adorn the Cottonera Lines

33. A painting by Matteo Perez d'Aleccio (c. 1547) depicting the assault on Fort St Michael. (A pontoon bridge to Fort St Angelo allowed for reinforcements and gave protection to the *Porto delle Galere*), and (*below*) part of the dungeon where galley slaves were kept when not straining at the oars

34. A rare photograph of the interior corridor in part of the Cottonera Lines built to defend The Three Cities

35. Grand Harbour showing the Castle of St Angelo and the Bighi Naval Hospital on the occasion of the Eucharistic Congress held in Malta in 1913. The numerous *dgħajsa*s are greeting delegates who attended the Congress from all over the world

36. St Anne's Gate leading to Senglea (*top*); and two of the many marble plaques pin-pointing places of interest in Birgu

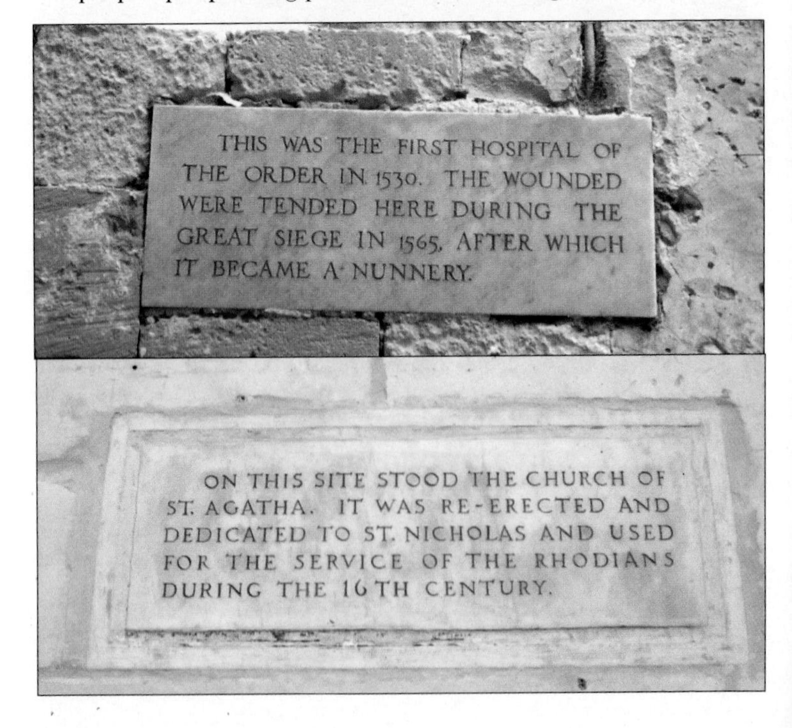

37. An impression by Joseph Goupy, of Cottonera with Cospicua in the foreground and Valletta in the background, during the reign of Grand Master de Rohan (1775-1797)

38. Three *dgħajsa*s competing in the 8th September Regatta held in Grand Harbour

39. The Church of St Margaret in Cospicua

40. The interior of the Church dedicated to the *Immaculate Conception*, Cospicua which became a Parish in 1586

41. The altarpiece of the Church painted by Peter Pȧul Caruana

42. A painting of *Our Lady with Child* by Francesco Zahra (1710-1773) in the Church of St Margaret, Cospicua

43. Part of St Edward's College, Cospicua, when used as a military hospital during the Gallipoli Campaign (1915-16) involving Britain in the war against the Turks

44. St James' Bastion in the Cottonera Lines

45. A portrait of Grand Master Nicolas Cotoner (1663-1680) who was responsible for the building of the Cottonera Lines which encircle The Three Cities

46. The Couvre Porte Gate

47. Two other gates leading into Vittoriosa

48. *The Three Cities*, a 19th century watercolour by Girolamo Gianni, an Italian artist who spent many years in Malta

Kalkara

Strictly speaking Kalkara is not part of Cottonera though it shared many of the vicissitudes of the Three Cities. It still retains aspects of an attractive fishing village and many of the island's traditional boats are repaired here.

Fort Ricasoli *(Cottonera map reference 1)*

Fort Ricasoli a large fortress at the mouth of the Grand Harbour is now used for the shooting of cinema films such as *Troy* and *The Count to Monte Cristo*. It was built in 1670 when Rafael Cotoner was Grand Master, and enlarged and strengthened by Grand Master Perellos (1697-1720). A small chapel in the Fort was dedicated to St Nicholas.

The British Administration used Ricasoli as a hospital when an epidemic of cholera broke out in 1837.

The Fort is not normally open to the public.

Fort Rinella *(map reference 2)*
(Bus no. 4 from Valletta. Open Monday to Saturday 10am to 4pm. Guided tours at 11.30am and 2.30pm. (Telephone 21809713). Entrance fee.)

A rare 100-ton gun, built by the British in the 19th century is at Fort Rinella in Kalkara. It is said to be the largest cannon in the world and its maker was the Victorian engineer Sir Williams George Armstrong of Newcastle. Only twelve guns of this calibre were ever made (there is one in Gibraltar), while a second one in Malta had been

Fort Ricasoli

sold for scrap. The cannon was capable of firing a one-ton shell a distance of three mils and piercing a 65cm of wrought iron armour. On Tuesday and Saturday at 2.30pm a re-enactment is held with volunteers dressed in Victorian military uniforms.

After years of neglect, Fort Rinella is being restored by a Heritage Foundation, *Fondazzjoni Wirt Artna*.

Rinella Movie Park

The Rinella Movie Park boasts one of the world's largest water tanks (Mediterranean Film Studios) and this is open to the public, May to October, on Wednesday to Sunday from 10am to 10pm. (*Entrance fee*)

Bighi Hospital

Although Bighi Hospital, in Kalkara, is named after the Italian knight, Bali' Fra Giovanni Bichi, the building was established as a British Naval Hospital at the insistence of Lord Nelson. Previously, the sick and wounded were housed in Birgu in what was known as the Armoury. In 1832 Bighi Hospital started to function; this had been built on the site of the villa and grounds belonging to the Bali' in an area known as *Tas-Salvatur* then forming part of Vittoriosa. During the brief French occupation, Napoleon Bonaparte intended to use the villa and its grounds as a new *Lazzaretto* for his troops. This did not come about since the French were forced out in 1801 and the British Naval Hospital was completed in 1832. The hospital closed down in September 1970, and is now used as a Discovery and Archaeological Resources Centre, partly as a seat for the Council of Science and Technology, and partly as a Centre for Restoration.

Jewish Cemetery in Kalkara

The remains of a Jewish Cemetery is to be found in Rinella Street, Kalkara, having been built there in 1784 by the 'Leghorn Fund' for ransoming Hebrew slaves. However, the first known Jewish burial grounds were near Rabat and date back to Roman times; and the first mention of a Jewish cemetery was in 1372 when King Frederick III granted

Bighi Hospital

some land at Tabia to the Jewish community. The site of this medieval Jewish cemetery was at 'Għariexem' near Mtarfa and was known as 'Qbur il-Lhud' – Jewish burial ground.

The Cemetery at Kalkara near St Joseph Square is some thirty by forty feet in area though it is believed to have been larger – in 1905 a German scholar gave the measurements as being forty by sixty feet. A document preserved at the National Library records that the Grand Master on application of Agostino Formosa de Fremeaux, 'agent for the Jewish Fund of Leghorn, grants the site and authority for the construction of a cemetery for burying Jews who die in his Dominion, on the shore of Salvatore Creek.' Today the cemetery contains twelve identifiable graves. Seven gravestones and one fragment are inscribed in Hebrew.

Żabbar

The Wickman Collection
(Dwardu Ellul Street, Żabbar)
A no. 21 bus from the Valletta terminus brings you to the Collection run privately, in Dwardu Ellul Street in the village of Xgħajra near Żabbar. Open by appointment. Telephone 21690254.

The Wickman Collection, in the vicinity of Kalkara, in Xgħajra, Żabbar, is privately owned and managed and has been committed, since 1950, to the preservation of maritime memorabilia. The aim is to illustrate the maritime scene especially during the British period 1815 to 1975. Particular attention is given to the development of maritime trade during the 19th century and to the close ties between Malta and the Royal Navy. It is interesting to note that during the reign of Grand Master de Rohan (1775–1797) Admiral Lord Hood secured the services of a number of Maltese seamen for the British Mediterranean Squadron. Included among the exhibits is the ship's binnacle from H.M.S. Magpie which was donated by the Duke of Edinburgh who commanded the ship and whose World War II battle honours include the Atlantic, Normandy and the Arctic.

The British and the Royal Navy came to Malta in 1814 and left in 1976.

Practical Information

Churches open for Services

Churches in the Three Cities tend to close early, and for those who wish to have a look inside at the many things of beauty which exist there, we have included a selective time table giving an indication when the Churches are celebrating Mass or holding other Services:

Vittoriosa (Birgu)

Parish Church of St Lawrence
Sunday and Feast Days: 6, 7, 8.30, 11am, 6pm
Saturday: 6pm
Daily: 4pm to 6.30pm

Church of the Annunciation
Sunday and Feast Days: 7, 8, 9, 10am and noon
Saturday: 6.15pm

St Scolastica
Sunday: 7am

Senglea(Isla)

Parish Church of the Nativity of Our Lady
Sunday and Feast Days: 7, 8, 9.15, 11am and 6pm
Saturday: 6pm
Daily: 6.30, 7.45 am and 6pm

St Philip
Sunday and Feast Days: 6.30, 8, 9.30am and 6pm
Daily: 8am and 6pm

Cospicua (Bormla)

Parish Church of the Immaculate Conception
Sunday and Feast Days: 6, 7, 8, 9.15, 11.45am and 5pm
Saturday: 4.45 and 6pm
Daily: 7 and 8.30am

St Margaret
Sunday and Feast Days: 7.15am
Daily: 7.15am

St Teresa of Avila
Sunday and Feast days: 6.45, 7.45, 8.45, 10.15am and 4.15pm
Saturday: 6.30pm
Daily: 6.15, 7.15 and 8am

Festa Days

If you enjoy colour, pageantry and fireworks, you may wish to attend one of the *Festas (Feast days)* in honour of the Patron Saint of the town or village. Those held in the Three Cities and in Kalkara are the following:

Vittoriosa (Birgu)

St Lawrence in mid-August (Buses 1 and 2)
St Dominic, late August

Senglea (L'Isla)

The Nativity of Our Lady – 8th September (Bus no 3)
Christ the Redeemer – late June

Dgħajsa in readiness for the 8th September Regatta

Cospicua (Bormla)

The Immaculate Conception – 8th December (Buses 1 and 2)

Kalkara

Feast of St Joseph – 13th July (Bus 4)

EATING OUT

Vittoriosa

CASINO DI VENEZIA

Vittoriosa Waterfront. Open Monday to Sunday 8pm to Midnight (closed on Tuesday). Reservations, telephone 21805580. (Take passport or ID card on your first visit)

BOCACCIO TRATTORIA

In the 18th century square next to the Couvre Porte Gate is the Bocaccio Trattoria where you can have a meal. Tuesday to Friday 11.30am to 2.30pm, Tuesday to Sunday, 7.30pm to 10.30pm (Telephone 21675757 and 79498600)

IL-FORN RESTAURANT

Il-Forn Restaurant in Triq it-Tramontana is housed in a 17th century building which includes work of arts. The owner is Austrian and his restaurant serves light Mediterranean dishes with a good choice of wines. Contact Clemans on telephone 21820379. Park your car in Victory Square, look out for a shop called Café de Brasil and walk along Hilda Tabone Street until you get to the second street on the right. Open on Wednesday to Saturday 7.30pm to 1am.

The number of eating places in Vittoriosa, Senglea and Cospicua is limited and it might be useful to list a few Restaurants to be found not far form the Three cities. Among these are:

Marsascala

GRABIEL

Situated in Mifsud Bonnici Square in Marsascala. Seating 65, this is a popular restaurant which specialises in fish. Air-conditioned. Telephone 21634194. Closed on Sunday.

LA FAVORITA

On the main Road – Gardiel street – this is a family run restaurant also serving fish dishes among others. Open Tuesday to Sunday. Telephone 21634113.

Marsaxlokk

IS-SAJJIED

This waterfront restaurant is in Xatt is-Sajjieda in Marsaxlokk. Open daily but closed for dinner on Sunday and closed on Saturday for lunch. Telephone 21652549.

Open Air Market

An Open Air Market is held every Tuesday morning in Cottonera Street leading to Cottonera Gate in Cospicua (Bormla)

LOCAL COUNCILS

***Vittoriosa* (Birgu)**
Couvre Porte. Telephone 21662166

***Senglea* (L'Isla)**
4th September Square. Telephone 21662424

Cospicua (Bormla)
2a St Margarita Street. Telephone 21663030

POLICE STATIONS

Vittoriosa
Triq Desain; Telephone 21825939

Senglea
4th September Square; Telephone 21826720

Cospicua
New Street (near St Helen's Gate); Telephone 21831239 and 21824218

Further Reading

Bugeja, Lino; Buhagiar, Mario; & Fiorini, Stanley – *Birgu (2 Volumes) – A Maltese Maritime City (1993)*

Blouet, Brian, *The Story of Malta (1967 & revised editions)*

Bradford, Ernle, *The Great Siege 1965 (1961);* and *Siege of Malta 1940-13 (1986)*

De Piro, Nicholas, *The International Dictionary of Artists who Painted Malta (2003)*

Fiott, Charles, *The Twin harbour Area (1994)*

Gambin, Kenneth, *The Inquisitors Palace, Vittoriosa (2003)*

Luke, Sir Harry, *Malta, An Account and Appreciation (1960)*

Monsarrat, Nicholas, *The Kappillan of Malta (1973)*

Trump, David, *Malta – Prehistory and Temples (2003)*

Schermerhorn, Elizabeth, *Malta of the Knights (1929)*

Zahra, Lorenzo, *Vittoriosa (1999)*

Appendices

SOVEREIGNS FROM 1090 TO 1530

NORMANS:

Roger (Count of Normandy)	1091-1101
Simon (Son of Count Roger)	1101
Roger II (Son of Count Roger)	1101-1154
William I (Son of Roger II)	1154-1166
William II (Son of William I)	1166-1189
Tancred I (Son of Roger II)	1189-1194
William III (Son of Tancred I)	1194

SUABIANS:

Constance (Daughter of Roger II and wife of Henry VI of the House of Hohenstaufen)	1194-1197
Frederick I (Son of Constance)	1197-1250
Conrad I (Son of Frederick I)	1250-1254
Conradin (Son of Conrad I)	1254-1266
Manfred (Natural son of Frederick I)	1266

ANGEVINS:

Charles of Anjou	1266-1283

ARAGONESE:

Peter I (III of Aragon)	1283-1285
James I (Son of Peter I)	1285-1296
Frederick II (Son of Peter I)	1296-1337
Peter II (Son of Frederick II)	1337-1342

Louis I (Son of Peter II)	1342-1355
Frederick III (Son of Peter II)	1355-1377
Mary I (Daughter of Frederick III)	1377-1420
Martin I (Husband of Mary I)	1402-1409
Martin II (Son of Martin and Mary)	1409-1412

CASTILLIANS:

Ferdinand I (Nephew of Martin II)	1412-1416
Alphonso I (Son of Ferdinand I)	1416-1458
John I (Son of Ferdinand I)	1458-1479
Ferdinand II (Son of John I)	1479-1516
Joanna I (Daughter of Ferdinand II)	1516-1518
Charles (Son of Joanna and Philip of Austria, Emperor of the Holy Roman Empire)	1518-1530

GRAND MASTERS OF THE ORDER OF ST JOHN IN MALTA

Philippe Villiers de L'Isle Adam (French)	1530-1534[6]
Pietro del Ponte (Italian)	1534-1535
Didier de Saint Jaille (French)	1535-1536
Juan de Homedes (Spanish)	1536-1553
Claude de la Sengle (French)	1553-1557
Jean Parisot de la Valette (French)	1557-1568
Pietro del Monte (Italian)	1568-1572
Jean l'Eveque de la Cassiere (French)	1572-1581
Hughes Loubenx de Verdalle (French)	1581-1595
Martin Garzes (Spanish)	1595-1601
Alof de Wignacourt (French)	1601-1622
Luis Mendez de Vasconcellos (Portuguese)	1622-1623
Antoine de Paule (French)	1623-1636
Jean Paul de Lascaris Castellar (French)	1636-1657

[6] In Rhodes from 1521.

Martin de Redin (Spanish)	1657-1660
Annet de Clermont de Chattes Gessan (French)	1660
Rafael Cotoner (Spanish)	1660-1663
Nicolas Cotoner (Spanish)	1663-1680
Gregorio Carafa (Italian)	1680-1690
Adrien de Wignacourt (French)	1690-1697
Ramon Perellos y Roccaful (Spanish)	1697-1720
Marc' Antonio Zondadari (Italian)	1720-1722
Antonio Manoel de Vilhena (Portuguese)	1722-1736
Ramon Despuig (Spanish)	1736-1741
Manoel Pinto de Fonseca (Portuguese)	1741-1773
Francisco Ximenes de Texadas (Spanish)	1773-1775
Emmanuel de Rohan Polduc (French)	1775-1797
Ferdinand de Hompesch (German)	1797-1798

CIVIL COMMISSIONERS, GOVERNORS and GOVERNORS-GENERAL

CIVIL COMMISSIONERS

Captain Alexander Ball, R.N.	1799-1801
Major-General Henry Pigot	1801
Sir Charles Cameron	1801-1802
Vice-Admiral Sir Alexander Ball, Bart.	1801-1802
Lieutenant-General Sir Hildebrand Oakes	1810-1813

GOVERNORS

Lieutenant-General the Honourable Sir Thomas Maitland	1813-1824
General the Marquess of Hastings	1824-1826
Major-General the Honourable Sir Frederick Ponsomby	1827-1836
Lieutenant-General Sir Henry Bouverie	1836-1843
Lieutenant-General Sir Patrick Stuart	1843-1847

The Right Honourable Richard More O'Ferrall	1847-1851
Major-General Sir William Reid	1851-1858
Lieutenant-General Sir John Gaspard le Marchant	1858-1864
Lieutenant-General Sir Henry Storks	1864-1867
General Sir Patrick Grant	1867-1872
General Sir Charles Van Straubenzee	1872-1878
General Sir Arthur Borton	1878-1884
General Sir Lintorn Simmons	1884-1888
Lieutenant-General Sir Henry Torrens	1888-1890
Lieutenant-General Sir Henry Smyth	1890-1893
General Sir Arthur Fremantle	1893-1899
Lieutenant-General Lord Grenfell	1889-1903
General Sir Mansfield Clarke, Bart.	1903-1907
Lieutenant-General Sir Henry Grant	1907-1909
General Sir Leslie Rundle	1909-1915
Field-Marshal Lord Methuen	1915-1919
Field-Marshal Viscount Plumer	1919-1924
General Sir Walter Congreve	1924-1927
General Sir John du Cane	1927-1931
General Sir David Campbell	1931-1936
General Sir Charles Bonham-Carter	1936-1940
Lieutenant-General Sir William Dobbie	1940-1942
Field-Marshal Viscount Gort	1942-1944
Lieutenant-General Sir Edmond Schreiber	1944-1945
Sir Francis Douglas (later Lord)	1945-1949
Sir Gerald Creasy	1949-1954
Major-General Sir Robert Laycock	1954-1959
Admiral Sir Guy Grantham	1959-1962
Sir Maurice Dorman	1962-1964

GOVERNORS-GENERAL

Sir Maurice Dorman	1964-1971
Sir Anthony Mamo	1971-1974

COMMANDERS-IN-CHIEF MEDITERRANEAN

1792	Samuel Granston Goodall	Rear Admiral
1793	Rt. Hon. Samuel Hood	Vice Admiral
1795	William Hotham	Admiral
1795	Sir John Jarvis	Admiral
1799	Rt. Hon. George, Lord Keith	Vice Admiral
1803	Rt. Hon. Horatio, Viscount Nelson	Vice Admiral
1805	Cuthbert Collingwood	Vice Admiral
1810	Sir Cotton Bart	Admiral
1811	Sir Edward Pellew	Vice Admiral
1814	Charles V Penrose	Rear Admiral
1815	Rt. Hon. Edward Lord Exmouth	Admiral
1818	Sir Thomas Freemantle	Rear Admiral
1820	Sir Graham Moore	Vice Admiral
1823	Sir Harry Neale	Vice Admiral
1825	Sir Edward Codrington	Vice Admiral
1833	Sir Pulteney Malcolm	Vice Admiral
1833	Sir Josias Rowley	Vice Admiral
1837	Hon. Sir Robert Stopford	Admiral
1841	Sir Edward Owen	Vice Admiral
1845	Sir William Parker	Vice Admiral
1852	James W Dundas	Rear Admiral
1854	Sir Edmund Lyons	Rear Admiral
1858	Arthur Fanshaw	Vice Admiral
1860	William Fanshaw Martin	Vice Admiral
1863	Robert Smart	Rear Admiral
1866	Rt. Hon. Lord Clarence Paget	Vice Admiral
1869	Sir Alexander Milne	Admiral
1870	Sir Hastings Reginald Yelverton	Vice Admiral
1874	Hon. Sir James R. Drummond	Admiral
1877	Geoffrey Phipps Hornby	Admiral
1880	Sir F. Blauchamp P. Seymour	Admiral
1886	H.R.H. The Duke of Edinburgh	Admiral
1889	Sir Anthony H. Hoskins	Admiral
1891	Sir George Tryon	Admiral
1893	Sir Michael Culme-Seymour	Admiral

1896	Sir John Ommaney Hopkins	Admiral
1899	Sir John Arbuthnot Fisher	Admiral
1902	Sir Compton E. Domville	Admiral
1905	Rt. Hon. Lord Charles Beresford	Admiral
1907	Sir Charles Carter Drury	Admiral
1908	Hon. Sir Assheton Gore Curzon Howe	Admiral
1910	Sir Edmond S. Poe	Admiral
1912	Sir A. Berkley Milne	Admiral
1914	Command in Abeyance (Sept 1914–Aug 1917)	
1917	Hon. Sir Arthur Gough Calthorpe	Admiral
1919	Sir John M. Derobeck	Admiral
1922	Sir Osmond De Beauvior Brock	Admiral
1925	Sir R.S.B. Keyes	Admiral
1928	Sir Frederick L. Field	Admiral
1930	Sir Ernle M. Chatfield	Admiral
1932	Sir William Wordsworth Fisher	Admiral
1936	Sir Dudley P.R. Pound	Admiral
1939	Sir Andrew B. Cunningham	Admiral
1942	Sir Henry H. Harwood	Acting Admiral
1943	Sir Andrew B. Cunningham	Admiral of the Fleet
1943	Sir john H. D. Cunningham	Admiral
1946	Sir Algernon V. Willis	Admiral
1948	Sir Ruther John Power	Admiral
1950	Sir John H. Edelsten	Admiral
1952	The Earl Mountbatten of Burma	Admiral
1955	Sir Guy Grantham	Admiral
1957	Sir Ralph Edwards	Admiral
1957	Sir Charles E. Lambe	Admiral
1959	Sir Alexander N. C. Bingley	Admiral
1961	Sir Derek Holland Martin	Admiral
1964-1967	Sir John Hamilton	Admiral

FLAG OFFICERS MALTA

1968	D.L. Davenport	Rear Admiral
1970	D.G. Kent	Rear Admiral
1972	J.A. Templeton-Cotill	Rear Admiral
1973	D.A. Loram	Rear Admiral
1975	Sir Nigel Cecil	Rear Admiral

BISHOPS OF MALTA SINCE 1530

Fra Balthasar Walkirk (German)	1530
Fra Tommaso Bosio (Italian)	1538
Fra Domenico de Cubelles (Spanish)	1540
Fra Martin Royas de Portalrubio (Spanish)	1572
Fra Tommaso Gargallo (Spanish)	1578
Fra Baldassare Cagliares (Maltese)	1615
Fra Giovanni Balaguer Camarasa (Spanish)	1635
Fra Lucas Bueno (Spanish)	1664
Fra Lorenzo Astiria (Spanish)	1668
Fra Michele Gerolamo Molina (Spanish)	1678
Fra Davide Cocco Palmieri (Italian)	1684
Fra Giacomo Cannaves (Spanish)	1713
Fra Gaspare Gori Mancini (Italian)	1721
Fra Paolo Alpheran de Bussan (French)	1728
Fra Bartolomeo Rull (Majorcan)	1758
Fra Giovanni Pellerano (Sicilian)	1770
Fra Vincenzo Labini (Italian)	1780
Fra Ferdinando Mattei (Maltese)	1807
Mgr Francesco Saverio Caruana (Maltese)	1829
Mgr Publio de' Conti Sant (Maltese)	1847
Mgr Gaetano Pace Forno (Maltese)	1857
Mgr Count Scicluna (Maltese)	1875
Mgr Antonio Buhagiar (Maltese) (Administrator)	1885
Mgr Sir Pietro Pace (Maltese)	1889
Mgr Angelo Portelli (Maltese) (Administrator)	1914

Mgr Dom. Maurus Caruana, O.S.B. (Maltese)	1915
Mgr Sir Michael Gonzi (Maltese)	1943
Mgr Joseph Mercieca(Maltese)	1976-

INQUISITORS IN MALTA

Mgr Pietro Duzzina	1574
Mgr Pietro Sant'Umano	1575
Mgr Rinaldo Corso	1577
Mgr Domenico Petrucci	1579
Mgr Federico Cefalotto	1580
Mgr Francesco Costa	1583
Mgr Ascnaia Libertano	1585
Mgr Gio. Batta Patralata	1587
Mgr Paolo Bellardito	1587,1590
Mgr Angelo Gennai	1590
Mgr Giovanni dell'Armi	1592
Mgr Innocenzi del Bufalo (afterwards Cardinal)	1595
Mgr Antonio Ortensio	1598
Mgr Fabrizio Verallo (afterwards Cardinal)	1600
Mgr Ettore Diottalevi	1605
Mgr Leonello della Carbora	1607
Mgr Evangelista Carbonesio	1609
Mgr Fabio Delagossa	1614
Mgr Antonio Torniello	1619
Mgr Paolo Torelli	1621
Mgr Carlo Bovio	1623
Mgr Onorato Visconte	1624
Mgr Niccolo Herrera	1627
Mgr Ludovico Serristori	1630
Mgr Martino Alfieri	1631
Mgr Fabio Chigi (later Pope Alexander VII)	1634
Mgr Gio. Batta Gori Pannellini	1639

Mgr Antonio Pignatelli (Pope Innocent XII)	1646
Mgr Carlo Cavalletti	1649
Mgr Federico Borromeo (afterwards Cardinal)	1653
Mgr Giulio degli Oddi	1655
Mgr Gerolamo Casanatte (afterwards Cardinal)	1659
Mgr Galezzo Mariscotti (afterwards Cardinal)	1663
Mgr Angelo Ranucci (afterwards Cardinal)	1666
Mgr Carlo Bichi (afterwards Cardinal)	1668
Mgr Giovanni Tempi	1670
Mgr Ranuccio Pallavicini (afterwards Cardinal)	1672
Mgr Ercole Visconti	1676
Mgr Giacomo Cantelmi (afterwards Cardinal)	1679
Mgr Innico Caraccioli	1683
Mgr Tomaso Ruffo	1686
Mgr Francesco Aquaviva (afterwards Cardinal)	1690
Mgr Giacinto Filiberto Ferreri	1698
Mgr Giorgio Spinola (afterwards Cardinal)	1703
Mgr Giacomo Caraccioli	1706
Mgr Ranieri Delic (afterwards Cardinal)	1711
Mgr Lazza Pallavicino	1718
Mgr Antonio Ruffo (afterwards Cardinal)	1720
Mgr Fabrizio Serbelloni (aftewrwards Cardinal)	1728
Mgr Gio Francesco Stoppani (afterwards Cardinal)	1731

Mgr Carlo Francesco Durni (afterwards Cardinal)	1735
Mgr Ludovicio Gualtieri (afterwards Cardinal)	1740
Mgr Paolo Pasionei	1743
Mgr Gregorio Salviati (afterwards Cardinal)	1754
Mgr Angelo Durini (afterwards Cardinal)	1760
Mgr G. Ott. Manciforte Sperelli (afterwards Cardinal)	1767
Mgr Antonio Lante (afterwards Cardinal)	1771
Mgr A.F. Chigi Zondadori (afterwards Cardinal)	1777
Mgr Alessio Falconieri	1785
Mgr Gio. Filippo Gallarati Scotti (afterwards Cardinal)	1785
Mgr Giulio Carpegna (afterwards Cardinal)	1793

(Mgr Carpegna went to Rome in 1798 and Rev. G.B. Gatt remained as Pro-Inquisitor. Two months later however, he was expelled by order of Napoleon Bonaparte.)

PRESIDENTS

Sir Anthony Mamo	1974-1977
Dr Anton Buttigieg	1977-1982
Miss Agatha Barbara	1982-1987
Mr Paul Xuereb (acting)	1987-1989
Dr Vincent Tabone	1989-1994
Dr Ugo Mifsud Bonnici	1994-1999
Professor Guido de Marco	1999-2004
Dr Edward Fenech Adami	2004-

PRIME MINISTERS OF MALTA

Senator Joseph Howard	1921-1923
Dr Francesco Buhagiar	1923-1924
Sir Ugo Mifsud	1924-1927
Sir Gerald (later Lord) Strickland, Count della Catena	1927-1932
Sir Ugo Mifsud	1932-1933
Dr (later Sir)Paul Boffa	1947-1950
Dr Enrico Mizzi	1950 (Sept-Dec)
Dr Giorgio Borg Olivier	1950-1955
Mr Dom Mintoff	1955-1958
Dr Giorgio Borg Olivier	1962-1971
Mr Dom Mintoff	1971-1984
Dr Carmelo Mifsud Bonnici	1984-1987
Dr Edward Fenech Adami	1987-1996
Dr Alfred Sant	1996-1998
Dr Edward Fenech Adami	1998-2004
Dr Lawrence Gonzi	2004-

Index

NOTES:

NOTES:

NOTES: